TECHNICAL REPORT

T0164189

Policy and Methodology to Incorporate Wartime Plans into Total U.S. Air Force Manpower Requirements

Manuel J. Carrillo, Hugh G. Massey, Joseph G. Bolten

TR-144-AF

August 2004

Prepared for the United States Air Force

Approved for public release; distribution unlimited

PROJECT AIR FORCE

The research reported here was sponsored by the United States Air Force under Contract F49642-01-C-0003. Further information may be obtained from the Strategic Planning Division, Directorate of Plans, Hq USAF.

Library of Congress Cataloging-in-Publication Data

Carrillo, M. J. (Manuel J.), 1949–
    Policy and methodology to incorporate wartime plans into total U.S. Air Force manpower requirements /
Manuel J. Carrillo, Hugh G. Massey, Joseph G. Bolton.
        p. cm.
    Includes bibliographical references.
    "TR-144."
    ISBN 0-8330-3581-9 (pbk. : alk. paper)
    1. United States. Air Force—Personnel management. 2. Manpower—United States. 3. Military planning—
United States. I. Massey, H. G. II. Bolten, J. G. (Joseph George), 1944– III. Title.

UG773.C37 2004
358.4'122'0973—dc22

                                                                                    2004006980

The RAND Corporation is a nonprofit research organization providing objective analysis and effective solutions that address the challenges facing the public and private sectors around the world. RAND's publications do not necessarily reflect the opinions of its research clients and sponsors.

RAND® is a registered trademark.

© Copyright 2004 RAND Corporation

All rights reserved. No part of this book may be reproduced in any form by any electronic or mechanical means (including photocopying, recording, or information storage and retrieval) without permission in writing from RAND.

Published 2004 by the RAND Corporation
1700 Main Street, P.O. Box 2138, Santa Monica, CA 90407-2138
1200 South Hayes Street, Arlington, VA 22202-5050
201 North Craig Street, Suite 202, Pittsburgh, PA 15213-1516
RAND URL: http://www.rand.org/
To order RAND documents or to obtain additional information, contact
Distribution Services: Telephone: (310) 451-7002;
Fax: (310) 451-6915; Email: order@rand.org

Preface

Manpower is a major component of the Air Force's capability to meet its designated wartime and peacetime missions. However, manpower requirements are also a major driver of costs in the Air Force budget. Periodically, the Air Force goes through an internal process that arrives at revised estimates of its manpower needs. The Total Force Assessment (TFA) carried out from 1999 to 2001 is the latest exercise (a process formerly known as FORSIZE) to examine the wartime and peacetime demands for Air Force capability and to estimate overall manpower requirements.

In 2000, Air Force Manpower and Organization (AF/XPM) asked the RAND Corporation to participate in the TFA. Robert Corsi, the deputy director at the time, emphasized the need for RAND to provide an independent assessment of the TFA process (later called TFA Phase I [TFA-I]) and its results, in addition to challenging assumptions while participating in the TFA. More recently, with the increased interest in sizing requirements for scenarios short of two major theater wars (MTWs), BGen Joseph Stein, while at AF/XPM, asked RAND to provide a requirements-estimating methodology that would accommodate scenarios not previously used in requirements determination; this work would be part of a TFA Phase II (TFA-II). This report, which documents the information briefed to Col William Bennett, AF/XPMR, in October 2001, serves as a response to both of these Air Force requests.

This report describes the new methodology that RAND proposed, which also uses some concepts that were part of the Air Force's TFA-I methods. We show how various Air Force policies and other alternatives affect requirements. Using Air Force data, this report also contrasts its requirements results for two-MTW scenarios with those TFA-I provided the Air Force. This comparison uncovered problems with TFA-I's requirements, tracing some to methodology and some to data problems. We also considered the Aerospace Expeditionary Force (AEF) environment to check the suitability of requirements for meeting the AEF's needs during peacetime to participate in small scale contingencies.[1] Our preliminary observation that authorizations appear adequate needs to be reviewed using

---

[1] At various times, the Air Force differentiates between the Expeditionary Aerospace Force (the "EAF environment") and the Aerospace Expeditionary Force (a 90-day rotational force). In this report, except for Section 5, we use only *AEF* for either case; the more precise meaning should be clear from the context.

more complete and current data, in light of the many changes in the AEF and its data systems that are on the way.

This report should be of interest to those concerned with manpower requirements, policy, methodology, and data. This study was conducted in RAND Project AIR FORCE's Manpower, Personnel, and Training Program.

RAND Project AIR FORCE

RAND Project AIR FORCE (PAF), a division of the RAND Corporation, is the U.S. Air Force's federally funded research and development center for studies and analyses. PAF provides the Air Force with independent analyses of policy alternatives affecting the development, employment, combat readiness, and support of current and future aerospace forces. Research is conducted in four programs: Aerospace Force Development; Manpower, Personnel, and Training; Resource Management; and Strategy and Doctrine.

Additional information about PAF is available on our web site at http://www.rand.org/paf.

Contents

Figures

Tables

Summary

Every few years, the U.S. Air Force reviews its authorized manpower to ensure that it has enough people with the right skills and experience to meet national security demands. During TFA-I, national security demands were expressed by the ability to prosecute two concurrent MTWs, a goal for defense planners at the time. As TFA-I drew to a close in 2001, that planning assumption was being reexamined as defense planners became increasingly interested in scenarios short of two MTWs.

TFA-I treated all existing deployable forces as being required for meeting a two-MTW threat. But because that is less likely with scenarios short of two MTWs, the Air Force found that it lacked a sanctioned method of estimating requirements for such diminished threats. As part of TFA-II, AF/XPM[1] asked RAND to provide a methodology that would fill this void. The principal purpose of this report is to summarize that methodology and illustrate its utility in application, i.e., to postulate demands for MTW-sized scenarios but less than two MTWs and estimate requirements on that basis.

RAND also participated, mainly as an observer, in TFA-I. We were given the opportunity to comment on the methodology along the way, which we did. At the end of TFA-I, RAND received from the Air Force copies of the TFA-I time-phased force and deployment data (TPFDD) and the TFA overall requirements file, which we analyzed while we developed our methodology for handling scenarios short of two MTWs. We tried to improve upon what we learned from our analysis of TFA-I methodology and results as we developed our new methodology.

We believe that the requirements methodology presented here is relevant regardless of the outcome of the debate on whether requirements estimation is necessary when the Air Force follows the capabilities-based concept. Our view is that the Air Force can achieve greater capability by efficiently trading-off resources to relieve bottlenecks. But feasible trade-offs are only possible when the locations of both the shortages and surpluses are known—in a word, requirements.

---

[1] That office has now become AF/DPM.

A More Broadly Applicable Methodology

For a given planning scenario, an estimation methodology for overall manpower requirements should be able to account for the following:

- How many positions of what kinds are needed to prosecute the conflict under consideration?

- How many additional positions of what kinds are needed to train the warfighters and otherwise sustain the peacetime force structure?

- How many additional base support positions are needed to sustain the warfighters?

Most Air Force combat and support personnel have both wartime and peacetime tasks. Proper estimation of requirements requires a methodology for tracking the peacetime workload that remains and the peacetime jobs made unnecessary by wartime jobs. In principle, *peacetime* jobs are tallied in the Manpower Data System (MDS)—the system that keeps track of authorized manpower by required Air Force Specialty Code (AFSC), authorized grade or skill, the Personnel Accounting Symbol (PAS), etc. The expected demand for *wartime* jobs depends on the wartime scenario. To provide greater specificity, war planners translate their postulated scenarios into the more-detailed TPFDDs.

As noted earlier, the most-important change in going from two-MTW scenarios to smaller MTW-sized scenarios is the possibility that not all current forces may need to be tasked in the smaller scenario. What to do with those untasked forces is a policy issue that needs to be considered outside the manpower modeling world. The conceptual framework and models we used for scenarios short of two MTWs are flexible enough to accommodate alternative policies for dealing with such untasked forces.

First, in our approach to requirements, we chose to follow the TFA-I concept that requires that each MDS manpower position be assigned to one of four categories, as determined by a manpower expert. We call this assignment the BIM classification. Since these categories resemble those used in TFA-I's Base Infrastructure Model (BIM), we refer to these as *BIM-like categories*. These categories are

- deployable forces, including deployable maintenance
- in-place combat forces (strategic nuclear forces, continental air defense, strategic airlift, space, missiles, etc.)

- continuing mission (field operating agencies, headquarters, depots, training, etc.)

- support, including base operating support (BOS).

To avoid double-counting (the rationale is given shortly), we also extend the BIM classification to the TPFDD demands.

Figure S.1 describes a special, illustrative case of our proposed requirements-estimation methodology. Some of the building blocks on the left (MDS broken into categories and hatched area TPFDD overlaid on top) will be selected in a "merge" to build the overall requirements on the right. To demonstrate its adaptability to alternative policies, we have described our methodology using an optional, theoretical overseas forward-presence requirements policy.

Unlike TFA-I, we do not move the entire building block of MDS deployable forces to the requirements column. Instead, we first set as requirements the MDS portion of deploying forces that we consider to be part of forward presence, those of USAFE and PACAF; then, we set as requirements the deployable forces in the TPFDD that are not part of USAFE or PACAF (see Figure S.1).

Next, as in TFA-I, we move the MDS in-place combat and continuing mission forces to the requirements column. Thus, we implicitly assume that the MDS positions in these two categories are sufficient to absorb any workload left behind by the corresponding positions in the TPFDD. TFA-I's two-MTW TPFDD data, for instance, are consistent with the assumption that few TPFDD forces fall into these two categories.

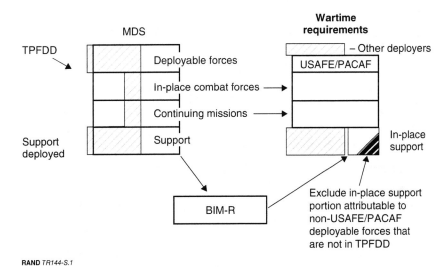

RAND TR144-S.1

**Figure S.1—Conceptual Modeling for an Overseas
Forward-Presence Requirements Policy**

Finally, we move only a portion of the support building blocks to the requirements column (Figure S.1), the deployable support for the TPFDD and the in-place support for the home base, which we estimated using our variant of BIM (BIM-R). RAND's BIM-R estimates in-place support by adjusting the MDS support positions to account for wartime's longer workweek and for workload changes arising from the departure of TPFDD deployers.

Because our BIM methodology uses all the support as input—including that for forces not used—we have to make one adjustment for the fact that this overseas-presence scenario may leave some forces unused (not all the deployable forces were moved to the requirements column). The effect of this additional adjustment is depicted in Figure S.1 as a dark triangle, which needs to be removed from the requirements for that scenario.

Observations on the Proposed Methodology

Neither TFA-I's approach nor ours estimates manpower requirements for every force and support function from first principles; that would be too massive an undertaking for a relatively small project.[2] Instead, both approaches focus on how to estimate changes to existing manpower requirements.

The resulting requirements are some combination of peacetime and wartime requirements. On the one hand, the requirements include the continuing mission category, which is a large block of MDS authorizations, the data system associated with Air Force peacetime requirements. On the other hand, the requirements include the deployable forces of a TPFDD.

A model similar to the BIM-like model that we used to handle the support BIM category could be useful for adjusting the continuing mission manpower category. Such a model could use a wartime workweek length to estimate the fraction of the continuing mission category that could be made available for, say, filling positions found to be short elsewhere.

Early in 2001, there was no official policy about how to handle untasked forces when the requirements goal is to meet some scenario short of two MTWs. The methodology we present allows the requirements model to exclude untasked forces from the requirements or to keep part of them, according to whatever policy the Air Force may present. Retaining forward-presence forces is an

---

[2] The Air Force has other ongoing processes that estimate peacetime requirements from first principles, such as those using manpower standards.

example of a possible policy statement. We feel that the proposed methodology is flexible enough to accommodate some other requirements policy statements.

When merging MDS and TPFDD positions into the overall requirements, avoiding double-counting hinges on consistent assignment of positions from the two files to appropriate BIM categories. Our proposed methodology extends the BIM classification to the TPFDD demands to deal with this potential problem. Our approach to assigning MDS and TPFDD positions to BIM categories achieves consistency by taking the organizational hierarchy implied by each unit's Personnel Accounting Symbol (PAS) and parent PAS codes into account. (See pp. 22–29.)

BIM-R pays special attention to the Reserve and Guard in an MTW-sized scenario where a full Reserve and Guard call-up occurs. For example, the BIM-R approach takes the peacetime part-timers' workload into account in determining how to meet the home-station workload in wartime. (See pp. 34–35.)

The excluded triangle in Figure S.1 is a first-order approximation. The proposed approach does not adjust other, related parts of the system, such as wholesale logistics (depots) and training.

Estimates Using the Proposed Methodology

The proposed methodology allowed us to estimate requirements for a variety of scenarios, including one for two MTWs and some for less-demanding scenarios. To demonstrate the methodology, we considered one-MTW scenarios (derived from the TFA two-MTW scenario), some small-scale contingency scenarios (as exemplified by vignettes), and the TFA two-MTW scenario itself. We then compared and analyzed the resulting requirements. In particular, it is possible to compare our results for the TFA's two-MTW scenario with the actual TFA results and to analyze their differences. (See pp. 42–48.)

We also performed one illustrative assessment under the "peacetime" EAF environment, in which most Reserve and Guard forces are part-timers. In this instance, we did not estimate requirements but, instead, used a capabilities-based Air Force view to check the adequacy of the two-MTW-based force structure for the peacetime EAF. This was an interesting case because, unlike the MTW scenarios we used for estimating requirements, the peacetime EAF is designed to function without a reserve call-up.

We compared manpower authorizations with actual personnel demand data to see whether the former were sufficient to satisfy the latter, by specialty and skill level. We were particularly interested in determining whether authorizations were sufficient to meet demand without exceeding corresponding deployment tour length limits for active or reserve personnel.

We found that, within the sample of specialties and skill levels we examined, the EAF authorizations could meet the great majority of demands within personnel tour length limits, even at peak demand. These authorizations failed to meet only a small percentage of the demands, inside or outside tour length limits. Thus, given the planning assumptions at the time, authorizations appear to have been adequate for meeting peacetime demand in the pre–September 2001 environment, although scheduling manpower resources may have presented some challenges. (See pp. 54–57.)

While analyzing requirements under the AEF, we noticed that there was no Air Force–wide policy on home-station workweek length, in contrast to MTW wartime planning, for which there is such a policy. A workweek length policy is necessary for estimating home-station requirements under AEF.

Lessons Learned from TFA-I and Suggestions for a Future TFA

Having familiarized ourselves with the TFA-I models, data, and process during our methodology development, we are able to offer some suggestions for a future TFA-like requirements exercise. We identified some important potential pitfalls in both the methodology and process TFA-I followed. There are indications in the TFA data that some of these potential pitfalls actually materialized in the TFA results. (See Appendix A.)

In the TFA-I methodology, the most serious potential pitfalls are related to double-counting in the merging of the MDS and the TPFDD to obtain the overall requirements. Our revised BIM classification methodology and our methodology in assembling requirements address these issues. (See pp. 22–29 and pp. 15–16.) We also suggest fully specifying the merge step's logic to allow greater degree of automation of the merge process. Additional automation would also provide the ability to fix merging errors quickly, as they are identified.

We suggest that the Air Force undertake a continuous effort to develop requirements-assessment and estimation models apart from those of TFA-like exercises. The short deadlines of TFA-like exercises make it impossible to develop a requirements methodology that can consider the various changes affecting the Air Force. It is likewise impossible to develop a methodology under such circumstances that would be adequate for considering alternative requirements policy options. Such an ongoing model development and assessment effort would allow a future TFA-like exercise to borrow the appropriate methodology for representing the requirements policies of interest, and reducing its model development and testing time.

The remaining observations have to do more with the TFA process. Given that one of the TFA goals was for its results to influence the program objectives memoranda, a new TFA-like process needs to have a more-careful set of controls, including quality controls. First, we suggest designating an organization to oversee quality control of the results and how they are used within the Air Force. The TFA-I process was geographically distributed in that it required that inputs be provided and a model (BIM) be run at the major commands (MAJCOMs) by the functional area managers (FAMs). A distributed process is inherently more difficult to control. The outcome of TFA-I was too sensitive to the varying degrees of success in communicating its goals and training its participants. The MAJCOM FAMs had wide authority to set support requirements levels, and there were few checks and balances. What incentives or disincentives did the FAMs have? Where were the accountability and auditing trails? We suggest providing incentives to the FAMs and MAJCOMs to encourage more efficient trade-offs of the manpower resources.

As one way to provide more controls, we suggest making the BIM classification process more extensive and methodical. A handful of manpower experts, fully accountable (as in our proposed methodology) at a central location would make an initial, default assignment of positions to BIM categories before the MAJCOM FAMs had the opportunity to revise or use them. FAMs would have to justify any overrides of the resulting defaults by producing appropriate documentation (and thus providing an auditing trail). We also suggest designing a mechanism for encouraging efficient resource trade-offs, such as setting upper bounds on budgets, on a functional or MAJCOM basis. Overall, we encourage developing more feedback summary reports throughout the process at the Air Force, MAJCOM, and functional levels to help identify and correct problems while the TFA-like process is in progress.

Acknowledgments

Understanding the Air Force's approach to manpower is a huge undertaking. We learned a lot about it from USAF participants to the TFA, many of whom have already been reassigned to other positions. Our ability to understand the approaches used in the TFA owes a great deal to Col Ray Conley and Maj Dave Crawford at AF/XPMR, Lt Col Kevin Ryan, William Tysinger, and Maj Ken Perry at AFMRF, and Lt Col Julia Gonzales at AFMIA. They included us in TFA meetings, giving us an insider's view.

We are also indebted to their staffs who answered numerous detailed questions about the Air Force methodology and data systems: TSgt Jeanne Schierhoff-Boone at XPMR, Capt Sandra Mayhall, Lt Sara Grossman, Lt Michelle Maffia, MSgt Eugene Blinn, and Thomas Ward at AFMRF, and MSgt John Blaquiere at AFMIA.

At AF/XOXW, TSgt Glen Littlefield shared with us his expert knowledge of TPFDD design. At the AEF Center, Col James Kippert and Walter Franklin shared their knowledge in AEF policy and data systems. Their help is gratefully acknowledged.

At RAND, we are thankful to Craig Moore, our RAND Project AIR FORCE program director at the time, for his confidence and support. Judy Mele processed Air Force assigned personnel data. Research communicator James Chiesa helped us provide more clarity and better order to the document.

We are indebted to the reviewers of this document who provided valuable observations and suggestions for its improvement.

In all cases, any errors or omissions found here remain our own.

Abbreviations

AEF	Aerospace Expeditionary Force
AEW	Air Expeditionary Wing
AFELM	Air Force Elements
AFMC	Air Force Materiel Command
AFMIA	Air Force Management and Innovations Agency
AFMRF	Air Force Manpower Readiness Flight
AF/DP	Deputy Chief of Staff, Personnel
AF/XO	Deputy Chief of Staff, Air and Space Operations
AF/XP	Deputy Chief of Staff, Plans and Programs
AFSC	Air Force Specialty Code
AFWUS	Air Force–Wide UTC Availability System
APOD	aerial port of debarkation
APOE	aerial port of embarkation
ARC	Air Reserve Component (includes the Reserve and Guard)
BFC	BIM Factor Calculator
BIM	Base Infrastructure Model
BIM-R	RAND's version of BIM
BOS	Base Operating Support
CME	Contractor Manpower-Equivalent (or Man-year Equivalent)
COB	collocated operating base
CONUS	continental United States
DMC	Deutsche-Mark and United Kingdom civilian
DRMD	Deployment Requirements Manning Document
DRU	Direct Reporting Unit
EAF	Expeditionary Aerospace Force
ECS	expeditionary combat support
FAC	functional account code
FAM	Functional Area Manager
FWE	[tactical] fighter-wing equivalent (assumed to consist of 72 aircraft)
FOA	field operating agency

GEOLOC	geographic location code
HQ	headquarters
IMA	Individual Mobilization Augmentee
JCS	Joint Chiefs of Staff
LCOM	Logistics Composite Model
MAF	manpower availability factor
MAJCOM	major command
MANFOR	Manpower Force Packaging
MDS	Manpower Data System
MOOTW	military operations other than war
MTW	major theater war
NEA	northeast Asia
ONW	Operation Northern Watch
OPLAN	operational plan
ORG	organization
OSD	Office of the Secretary of Defense
OSW	Operation Southern Watch
PAA	primary aircraft authorization
PACAF	Pacific Air Forces
PAS	personnel accounting symbol (includes the UIC)
P-MAF	peacetime manpower availability factor
POM	program objectives memorandum
RDD	required due date
SIGINT	signals intelligence
SIOP	Single Integrated Operational Plan
SOF	Special Operations Forces
SSC	small-scale contingency
SWA	southwest Asia
TDY	temporary duty
Tech	technician
TFA	Total Force Assessment
TPFDD	time-phased force and deployment data
UIC	unit identification code (see also PAS)
ULN	unit line number
USAF	U.S. Air Force
USAFE	U.S. Air Forces in Europe

UTC	unit type code
W-MAF	wartime manpower availability factor

1. Introduction

Every few years, the U.S. Air Force reviews its authorized manpower to ensure that it has enough people with the right skills and experience to meet national security demands. One of these exercises, the Total Force Assessment (TFA), was nearing its end in 2001. In previous years, the ability to prosecute the most-demanding two concurrent major theater wars (MTWs) had been a goal for defense planners and, thus, the goal of TFA Phase I's (TFA-I's) planning. In 2001, planners reexamined that assumption as interest increased in less-demanding scenarios.

TFA-I assumed that all existing deployable combat forces (as opposed to support) would be necessary for responding to a two-MTW threat. It does not, however, follow that this assumption would hold for scenarios short of two MTWs, or such scenarios would have no effect on planning. It is ultimately up to the Department of Defense (DoD) and the Air Force to decide what portion of the current deployable forces is necessary for meeting a specific threat.

Our research goal was to provide a methodological framework for identifying and providing the related manpower resources for the size of the force selected. When interest increased in estimating requirements for scenarios that are MTW-sized but short of two MTWs, the Air Force found itself without a sanctioned methodology or approach for making such estimates. So, as part of TFA Phase II (TFA-II), AF/XPM[1] asked RAND to provide the methodology to fill this void. The principal purpose of this report, then, is to summarize our methodology and demonstrate its usefulness through appropriate examples.

Note that participants in TFA-I were aware of the debate on whether requirements estimations are necessary in a capabilities-based Air Force. Perhaps because the participants were in the end sensitive to that debate, TFA-I's contributions can be characterized more as focusing on estimating changes in manpower requirements than on estimating requirements from first principles (see Section 2). As noted later, we borrowed some requirements concepts from the TFA-I methodology.

Our contention is that the requirements methodology, some of which is presented here, will continue to be relevant regardless of the outcome of the

---

[1] AF/XPM has since become AF/DPM.

debate on a capabilities-based Air Force. In economics (which is interested in limited resources), it is possible to make feasible and efficient (balanced) resource trade-offs only when one has information on the minimum resources necessary to attain a certain goal—in a word, requirements.

The next section begins by presenting requirements concepts and then gives an overview of TFA-I methodology and the steps of the process,[2] highlighting areas that can serve as motivation for our proposed methodology. Section 3 describes the requirements-estimation methodology that we propose, retaining as much of the TFA methodology as seems prudent. After an overview, we provide two extensive highlights of aspects of the methodology that we believe warrant special attention. The more-general requirements-estimation methodology proposed here also provides a broad framework for analyses of alternative scenarios. Section 4 applies the proposed methodology to the two-MTW threat and several less-demanding scenarios. We compare the resulting requirements with the positions currently authorized and with the requirements that TFA-I estimated.

We performed one additional illustrative policy assessment. We checked the adequacy of the two-MTW force structure for the peacetime Aerospace Expeditionary Force (AEF), which is manned without reservist call-ups. This analysis appears in Section 5. Section 6 presents concluding observations on our methodological contributions and offers some suggestions for improving future TFA-like exercises.

A secondary purpose of this document is to identify problematic aspects of the TFA and suggest improvements (i.e., enhancements in addition to those involved in generalizing the approach beyond the two-MTW scenario). We therefore allude to the TFA methodology and results in various places, particularly in Section 2, which provides an overview of TFA; in Section 4, which compares requirements; and in Section 6, which has our conclusions. Some of our comments on TFA are based on a detailed analysis of TFA input and output files, which appears in Appendix A.

Two things should be borne in mind while reading this report. First, the change in the threat since September 11, 2001, may ultimately require changes in the size and mix of Air Force manpower requirements, but planners are still debating

---

[2] We understand the word *process*, as the TFA guidance (HQ USAF XPMR, 2000b) uses it, to mean a project implemented by a set of tasks that follow a project management plan. Some of the tasks for the TFA-I process involved creating time-phased force and deployment data (TPFDD) specifications, classifying certain manpower data system (MDS) authorizations and running a model at various locations, reassembling data at a central location, and briefing results. Most tasks were performed by different people at different locations.

which direction to take. The methodology we propose here should be sufficiently flexible to accommodate requirements estimation for whatever policy is eventually chosen.

Second, the models this report presents are manpower models, as opposed to personnel models. Thus, they do not search for a preferred, sustainable grade mix. They accept the grade structures implicit in current deployer requirements and nondeployer authorizations and do not question whether these structures are sustainable. Once requirements are determined, personnel models would have to determine grade and year-of-service profiles sustainable under various accession and retention rate assumptions.

2. Manpower Requirements-Estimation Concepts and TFA-I

In this section, we begin by considering requirements estimation in general. Since the requirements methodology we propose is related to and tries to improve on that of TFA-I, we also present an overview of the latter as a basis for later comparison.

Overview

For a given planning scenario, an estimation methodology for overall manpower requirements must be able to account for the following:

- How many positions of what kinds are needed to prosecute the war?

- How many additional positions of what kinds are needed to train the warfighters and otherwise sustain the peacetime force structure?

- How many additional base-support positions are needed to sustain the warfighters?

Most Air Force combat and support personnel perform both wartime and peacetime tasks. To properly estimate requirements, a methodology is needed to track the peacetime workload that remains and the peacetime jobs made unnecessary by wartime jobs. In principle, peacetime jobs are tallied in the MDS—the system that keeps track of authorized manpower by Air Force specialty code (AFSC), functional account code (FAC), authorized grade or skill, the personnel accounting symbol (PAS), etc. To estimate peacetime requirements, the Air Force has used a variety of methods, including manpower standards that sometime depend on base population and programmed flying hours.

Expected demand for wartime jobs depends on the sizing scenario. To provide greater specificity in planning, the scenarios war planners postulate are translated into more-detailed TPFDDs.[1]

---

[1] The TPFDD is a list of unit type code (UTC) packages whose manpower composition is fully specified. TPFDDs focus on deploying forces but can contain in-place forces.

Once war planners choose the wartime scenario to use for setting requirements, the corresponding wartime requirements can be estimated,[2] along with the corresponding peacetime requirements. To get overall requirements, it is necessary to carefully merge some peacetime and wartime requirements, particularly avoiding double-counting the peacetime requirements that are subsumed under wartime requirements.

The Air Force's TFA-I

TFA's guidance document specified that the goal of TFA-I was "to estimate the Air Force's total manpower requirements for both peacetime and wartime operations" (Headquarters, U.S. Air Force [HQ USAF] XPMR, 2000b). The TFA-I can be characterized as a process (a project with many tasks and a project management plan). The guidance also stated that the results of TFA-I would influence the Quadrennial Defense Review, and program objectives memoranda and that its data would be used to respond to inquiries from Congress, the Office of the Secretary of Defense, and the Joint Chiefs of Staff (JCS). Furthermore, the guidance envisioned that the TFA wartime requirements would "populate the wartime file of the Manpower Data System" and would "provide data for use by Air Staff, MAJCOM/FOA/DRU [major command, field operating agency, or direct reporting unit], and base-level personnel for day-to-day management of manpower assets." Consistent with that, the TFA-I team designed the Base Infrastructure Model (BIM) to provide detailed requirements down to the level of individual positions.

To design the TFA-I methodology and an implementation "process," the TFA-I team had participants from Air Staff, in particular AF/XPMR; Air Force Manpower Readiness Flight (AFMRF); and the Air Force Management and Innovation Agency (AFMIA). The methodology involved the following steps:

- AF/XOPW[3] specified TFA-I's two-MTW TPFDD[4] (AFMRF, 2001b).

- MAJCOM functional area managers (FAMs) assigned each existing MDS manpower authorization to one of the four (BIM) categories, following TFA Guidance (HQ USAF XPMR, 2000b).

---

[2] The MDS actually includes some wartime requirements, most notably those directly related to flying and combat support aircraft. These may be derived from manpower standards based at least partially on the level of flying activity that the combat unit is to sustain in wartime.

[3] By 2002, AF/XOPW had become AF/XOXW.

[4] For brevity, we refer to this TPFDD as the *TFA TPFDD* or as the *TFA two-MTW TPFDD*.

- With the help of BIM, the MAJCOM FAMs estimated the "in-place support" requirements (for those authorizations classified as support).[5]

- AFMIA reassembled the MAJCOM BIM output data, and AFMRF and AF/XPMR merged it with other wartime requirements to arrive at what is referred to as "wartime file" requirements, while attempting to avoid double-counting positions.

Presumably, additional adjustments could be made at the end of the process to account for students, trainees, holdees, wartime attrition, etc., and even to accommodate AEF peacetime small-scale contingencies (SSCs). With the exception of the TPFDD and the final merging of data, the process took place on unclassified security systems.

As noted in the overarching guidance, the resulting requirements would be the total requirements for both peacetime and wartime operations.

TFA-I: BIM Classification of MDS Authorizations

As noted, the Air Force's TFA-I methodology required assigning each the MDS authorization to one of four categories:[6]

- deploying forces (both war-fighting forces and combat support)

- in-place combat forces (Single Integrated Operational Plan [SIOP], continental air defense, strategic airlift, space, missiles, etc.)

- continuing mission (FOAs/DRUs, headquarters, depots, training, etc.)

- in-place support, including base operating support (BOS) inside and outside the CONUS.

We refer to these categories as the BIM categories because of their relationship to that model, which TFA-I used to estimate the in-place support requirements (AFMIA, 2000).

To facilitate assignment to BIM categories, and understanding that the TFA TPFDD would include all aviation UTCs, the TFA guidance included a list of only 33 organization kind and type pairs that could be presumed (if not in-place combat units) to be in the deploying forces category (HQ USAF XPMR, 2000b, Appendix 7), but it also provided a more-comprehensive suggested list of the

---

[5] A MAJCOM FAM would run the BIM for its functional area for all the bases in that MAJCOM.

[6] Early in TFA-I, the category *in-place combat forces* was called *in-place forces*, while *continuing mission* was called *directed mission*.

organizations in the continuing mission category (HQ USAF XPMR, 2000b, Appendix 5). The TFA guidance did not provide a comparable list for in-place support.

A Conceptual Model of the Requirements-Estimation Methodology of TFA-I

The TPFDD (hatched area in Figure 2.1) is likely to include some of the in-place combat forces and continuing-mission forces. It also includes deploying forces and deployed base support. Although not emphasized during TFA-I, its TPFDD could, in principle, further specify forces and support that are not currently authorized and thus are not in the MDS (the heavy black-line rectangles in Figure 2.1). Depending on additional assumptions, the total requirement (here and in the following figures) is a subset of manpower falling within the hatched area and the outlined white area, counting what falls in the overlap between the two areas only once.

Requirements estimation is a big job because of the Air Force's sheer size. Not counting students, trainees, and holdees, the Air Force's MDS for the fourth quarter of FY 2001 (dated June 2000) listed about 330,000 (unclassified) authorized military positions in the active component. The number reached about 636,000 when one included Air Force Reserve, Guard, and civilians.[7] The TFA's approach, review, and reestimation of manpower requirements focused on the scenario's war plans or TPFDDs and on the support category and, in general, paid less attention to the continuing mission category.

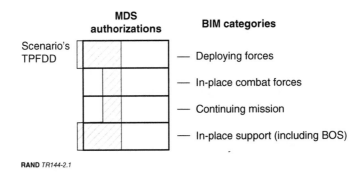

RAND TR144-2.1

Figure 2.1—Manpower-Requirements Building Blocks and BIM Categories

---

[7] This report does not take contractor manpower equivalents (CMEs) into account (see Appendix D for other exclusions).

We now take up each of the BIM categories and describe how TFA-I infers requirements from the TPFDD and MDS authorizations. As Section 1 explained, TFA-I used the most-demanding two-MTW scenario (AFMRF, 2001b) for sizing requirements. When depicting the assessment's methodology, the TFA-I charts included all the MDS deploying forces authorizations as requirements. We represent this in Figure 2.2 by "moving" the MDS deploying forces over to the right side of the figure (Wartime requirements).

The second step assumes that all in-place combat forces and continuing-mission authorizations in the MDS are required (see Figure 2.2). Any part of these that is tasked in the TPFDD is not added a second time to the requirements; MDS positions in these categories are assumed to be sufficient to cover any such TPFDD demand.[8] TFA-I assumed that the extra man-hours resulting from the longer Air Force workweek in a two-MTW scenario would compensate for any shortfalls that meeting deployment demands in these two categories might cause at their home bases.

Now, we turn to the final step in assembling manpower requirements. Because the TPFDD includes some support (the deploying support manpower), that portion of the support, like the deploying forces themselves, needs to be moved to the requirements column (the lower hatched rectangular area in Figure 2.2). In addition, the bases must have enough manpower in the support category to support the forces or other mission manpower remaining there. For this, TFA-I

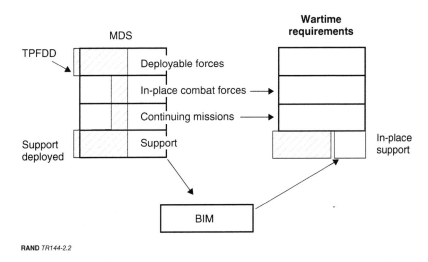

RAND TR144-2.2

Figure 2.2—Overview of TFA-I's Requirements Methodology

---

[8] Under TFA-I, there was no mechanism for assigning each of the TPFDD positions to BIM categories. In our proposed approach, we used a method that resulted in 11 percent of the TFA TPFDD positions in the in-place combat forces or continuing mission categories (see Section 3).

used present support authorizations after adjustments to them were made by using the BIM.[9] This model adjusts to account both for wartime's longer workweek (related to the wartime manpower availability factor [MAF]) and for workload changes arising from the departure of deploying personnel. This would typically reduce the requirement, as the size of the lower unhatched rectangular area on the right side of Figure 2.2 relative to that on the left indicates.

Section 3 describes BIM methodology in more detail, as well as that of a comparable model, RAND's BIM-R.

Observations on TFA-I

The rest of this section offers some observations on TFA-I that we based mostly on a qualitative analysis of its assumptions, methodology, and process. The focus is on relevance to the methodology improvements we present in later sections.

The TFA Two-MTW TPFDD

Specifying what combat forces or aviation resources are required to prosecute a two-MTW conflict is outside the scope of a manpower requirements methodology. AF/XOPW built the TFA TPFDD with the understanding that TFA's two MTWs would need all available aviation units: That, by itself, made that TPFDD special. It was also special in that it was not checked for transportation feasibility. The TFA TPFDD included not only deploying units but also many in-place combat forces.

For example, the TFA TPFDD used all 20 of the Air Force's (tactical) fighter-wing equivalents (FWEs). Of these, eight (identified by a special code in the TPFDD file) had some sort of unknown destination. We could not determine whether the eight FWEs were intended to be on-call reinforcements or reserves because, unlike most TPFDDs, the required due date (RDD) data field had been omitted, along with any other timing information.[10]

TPFDDs, including that for TFA, typically consist of lists of UTC packages (more on this later) sourced (tasked) to existing units. Linking a TPFDD, which affects manpower requirements, to existing units and their resources highlights the

---

[9] Past FORSIZE efforts to estimate manpower requirements required a lot of manual effort. In TFA-I, BIM partially automated estimation of in-place support requirements.

[10] The rationale for not having an RDD was that the TFA TPFDD included only the demands for the sustainment period.

dependence of TPFDDs on current authorizations; a de facto mechanism for making a TPFDD independent from authorizations is not to source parts of it, which happened for some TFA TPFDD demands. In any case, TPFDDs are limited by the number of aerospace systems (aircraft) and other manpower-associated TPFDD-related equipment, for which additional numbers require procurement (equipment) outside the manpower arena.

The sourcing of a TPFDD also affects the resulting force mix of active, Reserve, Guard, military, or civilian manpower. Few civilians are included in current TPFDDs. This seems appropriate for deployments to locations where personnel may see combat but may overly constrain the mix for forces that operate from the continental United States (CONUS) or USAFE in support of MTWs elsewhere. This is relevant because TPFDDs, including the TFA TPFDD, include some in-place combat forces. The mix in a TPFDD, or its associated overall requirements, therefore depends on the mix of the existing force and is not optimized during the requirements-estimation process. A separate analysis seems required to assess alternative force mixes.[11]

The Peacetime Authorizations, the TPFDD, and Merging Them to Arrive at TFA Wartime Requirements

From the description of its methodology, what TFA-I calls wartime requirements almost looks like a merging of peacetime and wartime requirements to create a set of overall requirements. For example, TFA-I assumed that large blocks of authorized nondeployer positions are required.[12] One could easily envision adjusting the continuing mission manpower category using a model similar to the BIM, which currently affects only the support category; such a model could use a wartime workweek length to estimate the fraction of the continuing mission category that could be made available for, say, filling required positions elsewhere.

In any case, the TFA methodology cannot be characterized as estimating requirements from first principles, as perhaps could be said of methods that use Air Force manpower standards or even the Logistics Composite Model (LCOM). Instead, TFA-I is better characterized as a process for estimating changes in overall requirements.

---

[11] The two-MTW TPFDD in TFA-I provided by the Air Force is not suitable for a force mix analysis because it lacks an RDD field (an important parameter for determining whether the Reserve or Guard could be used).

[12] These blocks include about 169,500 MDS continuing mission positions, as TFA-I classifies them.

At first glance, this merging of peacetime requirements (as represented by the MDS authorizations) and wartime requirements (as represented by the TFA TPFDD) would seem to be clever. However, a potential pitfall of the approach is that it hinges on identifying and tracking during the process of merging not only MDS but also TPFDD positions in the Support category. However, TFA-I made no explicit attempt to assign each TPFDD position to a corresponding BIM category at the same time it was classifying the MDS authorizations. As is discussed in Appendix A, difficulties in identifying TPFDD support led to important problems in the merge of peacetime and wartime requirements.

The TFA Process

As noted in Section 1, the MAJCOM FAMs—through a geographically distributed process—performed the BIM classification of MDS authorizations and, for support, provided inputs and ran the BIM to estimate in-place support. BIM, a variation of which is discussed in Section 3, provided the methodology in estimating in-place support requirements. From the Air Force's perspective, the participation of the MAJCOM FAMs in the MDS classification and the distributed running of the BIM were desirable so that the resulting overall requirement would have the support of the MAJCOMs. Participation of the MAJCOM FAMs was attractive because they can be considered the experts in a given functional area and because the FAMs already had a functioning organization in place, both at the MAJCOMs and at the Air Staff.

However, one could easily imagine that it could be difficult to control TFA-I's distributed process for running the BIM, even under the best of circumstances. First, the participants required time-consuming training, which had to be—at least for the large MAJCOMs—scheduled sequentially. Then, the FAMs had varying degrees of success in understanding and following the guidance consistently. In particular, quality control is important when the results that will emerge from a process will influence the POM. Our review of the process, however, indicated that the controls were not explicit and that the auditing trail was inadequate (more on this in Appendix A).

An important drawback in the TFA-I process was that it had to go through most of a lengthy process before it became clear what the merged, Air Force–wide peacetime and wartime requirements would look like. This was true even though the MAJCOM FAMs could check their classifications of MDS positions and how BIM was working by looking at BIM results for their MAJCOM and function. When problems became apparent when viewing Air Force–wide summaries after merging results, it would have been untenable to modify the process, go through the additional training required, rerun the BIM, and then merge the peacetime and wartime requirements.[13]

In the next few sections, we propose a methodology that would improve on some of the TFA limitations we have mentioned and that will thus benefit any future TFA-like efforts.

---

[13] TFA-I had its own project deadlines. Furthermore, along the way, it was decided that the TFA results were to be used in the Total Force Career Field Review (TFCFR), which imposed additional deadlines.

3. A More Broadly Applicable Methodology for Manpower Requirements

This section sets out the methodology we propose for estimating manpower requirements for a variety of MTW-sized demand scenarios, including two or short of two MTWs. For the two-MTW case, it provides improvements over the methodology TFA-I used. We begin with an overview that summarizes our approach, contrasting it to that in TFA-I. We then show the flexibility of the approach by demonstrating how it accommodates some alternative requirements policies. We then highlight two aspects of the methodology that warrant a more-detailed presentation: assigning manpower to BIM categories and estimating in-place support.

A Conceptual Model of the Proposed Requirements Estimation Methodology

To estimate the manpower requirements, we first perform a BIM-like classification,[1] i.e., we assign not only each MDS authorization but also each TFPDD position to one of the following four categories:

- deployable forces, including deployable maintenance[2]

- in-place combat forces (SIOP, continental air defense, strategic airlift, space, missiles, etc.)

- continuing mission (FOAs, DRUs, headquarters, depots, training, etc.)

- support, including BOS.

Although these category names sound similar to the four BIM categories for TFA-I (presented in the last section), there are differences. Note that the first category is *deployable*, rather than *deploying*, forces; this category includes the combat support most directly connected to the flying forces but excludes deployed base BOS. Forces in this category are deploying for some scenario but not necessarily the one under consideration.

---

[1] For brevity, we also call it a *BIM classification*.

[2] The deployable forces a TPFDD includes are called *deployers*; they include combat units.

We also have a separate category for support; this category includes BOS when it is part of the MDS and may include deployed support when it is part of the TPFDD. The MDS authorizations in the support category are used to estimate "in-place support:" Support authorizations are adjusted with the help of FAM inputs and a modified BIM (model), which we refer to as the RAND BIM (BIM-R). We refer to these categories as *BIM-like categories*. We describe these categories in greater detail later in this section and compare the resulting classifications to those used in TFA-I in Appendix B.

Just as we did in Section 2 for TFA-I, we can take up each of the BIM categories and describe how we infer requirements from the MDS authorizations and the TPFDD. As previously noted, TFA-I's approach, as a matter of policy, treated all the deployable forces as requirements. However, if the resulting requirements for scenarios short of two MTWs are to be any different from those for two MTWs, such a policy cannot apply in general. This is a fundamental issue that we will treat shortly. For now, as Figure 3.1 illustrates, the first step in assembling manpower requirements is to assume that only the deployable forces listed in the TPFDD are deployable requirements.

The second step assumes that all in-place combat forces and continuing-mission authorizations in the MDS are requirements. This is the same way that TFA-I handled them, and it is subject to the same comments that we made in this regard in the previous section.

The final step in assembling manpower requirements has also changed from that of TFA-I. As in TFA-I, the deploying support manpower of the TPFDD needs to be "moved over" to the "requirements column" (the lower hatched rectangular area in the right side of Figure 3.1). Now, BIM-R does the estimation of the support required for a base's remaining force or other mission manpower. This model adjusts the present support authorizations to reflect both wartime's longer workweek and the workload changes arising from the departure of deploying personnel. More important for scenarios short of two MTWs, the support requirement needs to be trimmed by excluding support for deployable forces not used in the present scenario (as shown in Figure 3.1; this exclusion takes place outside BIM-R). We describe this BIM-R and related adjustments further below; it provides model enhancements over the BIM used during TFA-I.

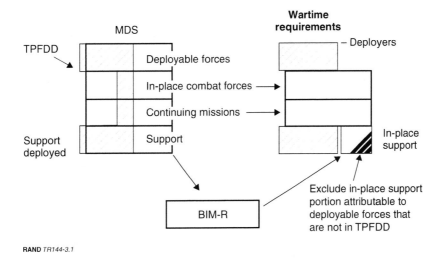

RAND *TR144-3.1*

**Figure 3.1—Overview of Proposed Methodology to Estimate
Manpower Requirements**

Observations on the Proposed Methodology

TPFDDs

The proposed methodology is designed to accept any TPFDD, in particular a
TPFDD corresponding to a scenario short of two MTWs.

What to Do with Untasked Forces

The proposed methodology does not deal with the policy issue of whether the
force structure should exclude the forces the specified TPFDD does not task. The
number and size of these untasked forces might be such that removing them
from the force structure might require major changes in basing and support. If
that were the policy, the proposed methodology could indicate areas in wings
suitable for minimum cutbacks, but the methodology would not even attempt to
estimate the cutbacks required in training, wholesale logistics and maintenance
(e.g., depots), etc. Using the proposed methodology does make it clear that
keeping all untasked forces at their bases while some of the bases' support is
deployed may mean that the home-station support requirements for the
untasked units may cause the new overall support requirements to be greater
than those required in peacetime. This result is disconcerting but accurate when
fewer wartime requirements require greater home-station support requirements,
some for untasked forces.

Note the manpower requirements policy apparently does not indicate what to do with untasked forces in scenarios short of two MTWs. The methodology we present is flexible enough to accommodate possible requirements policy in this area, such as the hypothetical policy for overseas forward presence. Later in this section, we will discuss how to use the proposed methodology to handle such policies.

The Peacetime and Wartime Requirements and Merging Them into the Overall Requirements

As with the TFA-I methodology, it is better to characterize our methodology as a way to estimate changes in overall requirements rather than to estimate peacetime or combined peacetime and wartime requirements from first principles.

Later in this section, we show that our methodology provides a structure to the BIM classification of TPFDD and MDS. This ultimately improves on the TFA-I methodology by avoiding double-counting of positions when merging peacetime and wartime requirements.

A Revised TFA Process Using the RAND Methodology

An important feature of TFA-I was that MAJCOM FAMs performed the BIM classification of MDS authorizations and either provided the inputs to the BIM or actually set the final in-place support requirements. The drawbacks of that part of TFA-I were the length and weak quality control of the process.

To address the drawbacks noted, we envision a process designed to be carried out not at the MAJCOMs but in the more controlled environment of an analysis unit. The manpower analysts there would use the structure in the proposed methodology as this section describes later, along with expert judgment, to select a default BIM classification of MDS and TPFDD demands based on the unit's formal organization kind and type. These initial assessments would be treated as the default by everybody else, unless a formal case for change could be made by others. Then, BIM-R, which treats Reserve and Guard units more carefully than BIM does, would be run by the analysts to estimate in-place support.

The initial resulting in-place support and overall requirements results (excluding security-classified portions) could then be published through a web site, which the MAJCOM FAMs would use to request revisions to the BIM-like (MDS and TPFDD) classification defaults, but staying within the BIM-R classification constraints described later in this section. These requests would have to supply supporting documentation to provide an auditing trail. The constraints enforced in the BIM classification make it easier to automate the merging of peacetime and wartime requirements to obtain the overall requirements. Greater automation also makes it possible to accept multiple revisions from FAMs.

Responding to Alternative Requirements Policy and Avoiding Double Counting

Some variations from the two-MTW scenario may not require all the current forces. Some combat forces not explicitly tasked in a TPFDD may still be needed for other purposes, as dictated by policy. Our approach allows for different manpower requirements, depending on the selected policy.

For example, as noted earlier, TFA-I used the most-demanding two-MTW scenario for sizing requirements (AFMRF, 2001b). Its policy was to treat all deployable manpower as requirements. Figure 3.2 shows the results of applying our approach to the TFA-I two-MTW scenario. In this case, there are no "unused" deployable forces (and no TPFDD deployable forces required in excess of authorizations). Consequently, it is not necessary to adjust in-place support by deducting the support slice that goes with unused deployable forces.

Another policy might choose a forward presence overseas. Such a policy might require retaining all deployable forces in the USAFE and PACAF MAJCOMs, even if they were not tasked in the TPFDD for a scenario less demanding than two MTWs. Figure 3.3 depicts the corresponding requirements.

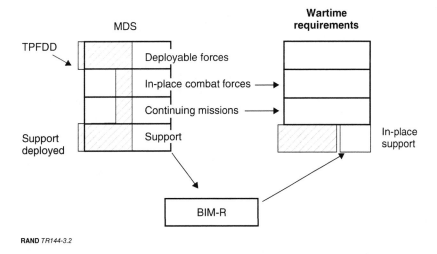

RAND TR144-3.2

Figure 3.2—Conceptual Modeling for TFA-I's Requirements Policy

20

The policy Figure 3.3 assumes is particularly useful for illustrating how requirements estimation can be prone to double-counting, i.e., counting both the TPFDD demand and the MDS position that fills it as separate requirements. To help avoid that, our approach mandates assigning the TPFDD demand (not just the MDS authorizations) to BIM categories. This should eliminate double-counting within the in-place combat forces and continuing mission categories, because TPFDD demands in these categories are not added to the requirements column. The other two categories, however, are another matter, and for them we describe our approach more carefully below.

We have discussed three requirements policies governing which *deployable* forces become part of requirements:

a. all TPFDD deployable forces (Figure 3.1)

b. all MDS deployable forces (Figure 3.2)

c. non–forward-presence TPFDD deployers and overseas forward-presence MDS deployable forces (Figure 3.3).

The first two policies avoid double-counting because either the TPFDD deployables or the MDS deployables, but not both, move to the requirements column. However, as illustrated in Figure 3.3 for the forward-presence scenarios, the methodology for estimating requirements under the third policy depends on identifying a unit's MAJCOM. MDS authorizations (and sourced TPFDD demands) have units, each identified by the four-character Personnel Accounting

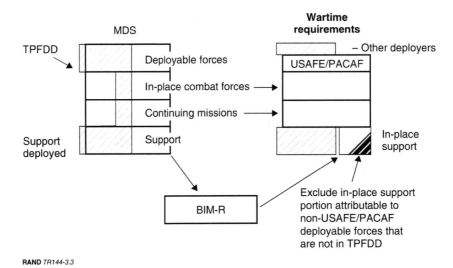

RAND TR144-3.3

**Figure 3.3—Conceptual Modeling of Requirements for a
Forward Presence Overseas**

Symbol (PAS) or Unit Identification Code (UIC) whose MAJCOM can be looked up in a PAS table. MDS deployable force authorizations in USAFE and PACAF count toward the requirement (top white rectangle on the right in Figure 3.3). For deployable forces not in USAFE/PACAF, we include only the deployable force requirements from the TPFDD (top hatched area on the right in Figure 3.3). The MAJCOM cannot be determined for the unsourced TPFDD demands, i.e., those for which the TPFDD specifies no PAS.[3] For unsourced demands, we imputed the MAJCOM to be *Other* in the active component but different from USAFE or PACAF.[4] If our imputation was erroneous and the demand's MAJCOM actually was USAFE or PACAF, we would presumably be double-counting a unit already in the MDS. Such double-counting can be avoided only when the Air Force sources each TPFDD demand to a unit. Adapting our approach to other requirements policies would similarly require sufficient sourcing data to avoid double-counting.

Highlight 1: Classification of Manpower

We suggest that the reader browse the remainder of this section on a first reading and then come back and read it in more detail after Section 4.

Our methodology requires a system that assigns manpower positions to one of the BIM categories, whether the position is part of the MDS authorizations or of the TPFDD demand. This subsection describes, in some detail, the logical structure in this classification for each of these data sources. We begin by defining the categories more thoroughly than we did earlier.

Proposed BIM Categories

The four categories resemble those in TFA-I. The classification system can initially be thought of as applying to organizational units, but we also allow the classification to apply to work centers within a unit, identified by the FAC.

- *Deployable forces* are those whose primary wartime mission is (or is expected to be) to deploy to combat theaters as combat or combat support elements. These include all aviation and maintenance units that do not have specific in-place missions. We also include aerial port units, aeromedical evacuation

---

[3] In the TFA TPFDD, 9,329 positions are unsourced, or approximately 4 percent. Most of them are in the support area (see Table A.2), but 8 percent are in maintenance.

[4] The "bite" out of the upper hatched area in Figure 3.3, immediately to the left of the USAFE/PACAF rectangle (compare the left and right sides), reflects our assumption that no unsourced TPFDD deployable forces elements are associated with USAFE/PACAF.

units, RED HORSE civil engineering squadrons, and other units that fall outside the areas of aviation and maintenance or of base support but that are deployable and do not have in-place wartime responsibilities. For example, aerial port units on strategic airlift bases are treated as in-place combat forces, but those on C-130 or other tactical airlift bases are considered deployable forces.

- *In-place combat forces* include strategic airlift, continental air defense, SIOP elements, and other units whose primary wartime mission would be conducted from their home bases.

- *Continuing-mission* units are in-place elements, such as Air Force and MAJCOM headquarters units, FOAs and DRUs, and training, depot maintenance, and development and acquisition units.

- *Support* includes wing or base units whose primary missions are to support the wing or group structure and to provide host BOS to all base tenants.

Using Personnel Accounting Symbols to Categorize Authorizations

It is of utmost importance to assign manpower positions to the correct BIM categories. If a manpower position is classified as support, it may be subject to adjustments for wartime's longer workweek and the change in workload due to changes in the base's mission population. Incorrect support classifications could thus result in an incorrect total requirement. We developed a system for assigning manpower to BIM categories using a rational and consistent initial set of classification defaults that can later be overridden only by selected authorized personnel, if an explanation is provided.

Each manpower position, whether in the MDS or a sourced TPFDD, is associated with a PAS code (from which one deduces the organization [ORG] number, kind, and type) and a (four-character) FAC. Our BIM classification system uses these PAS codes and FACs. The default classification system is rational because it uses the unit hierarchy implied by the PAS and its parent PAS code for each unit in the MDS. Overall, our approach can classify authorizations on the basis of the unit's characteristics, the MAJCOM deduced from the PAS, and the FAC. In arriving at the present classification, we tried to incorporate any patterns that could be identified from TFA BIM output files. For example, service squadrons were almost always treated as in-place support in TFA-I, so we followed suit. For a quantitative comparison of our classification of MDS authorizations with that from TFA-I, see Appendix B.

The PAS-implied hierarchy characterizes the relationship of units on each base.[5] It is used to identify, for example, which maintenance units provide maintenance for a given flying squadron. The hierarchy also facilitates performing certain tasks outside BIM-R, e.g., identifying support other than base support.[6] Because base experts may have additional information not derivable from the PAS hierarchy or unit and FAC information in the MDS, they may need to override our default classification. The MAJCOM FAMs, who ran the BIM during TFA-I, may be presumed to be experts in their MAJCOM bases. However, some are bound to be new to their jobs and need help in making the necessary BIM input choices (e.g., BIM classification). Requiring documentation of deviations from the default classification will generate an auditing trail that can only strengthen the credibility of the subsequent BIM results. We propose that such a full audit trail be provided.

One of the principal lessons we learned in constructing our BIM classification system for the MDS is that it need not be a monumental task. Tables 3.1 and 3.2 suggest that such a classification is necessary for only a modest number of organizations. First, for many authorizations, knowing only the two-character ORG type is enough information to permit BIM classification. Table 3.1 is a partial list of ORG types deemed to be continuing missions.

The 15 ORG types listed in Table 3.1 plus another 35 ORG types related to ORG kinds beginning with the letters q (various ORG types), x, and z (Air Force elements [AFELMs]) are assigned to the continuing mission BIM category; these 50 ORG types already cover 452 of the ORG kind–ORG type pairs present in the MDS we considered. Such assignments determine the BIM classification for 102,540 MDS authorizations.[7] Refer to Table 3.2.

Similarly, for many authorizations, knowing only the three-character organization kind and two-character type is enough information to permit the BIM classification. For example, recruiting squadrons (ORG kind "rec," type "sq") include many PAS codes, but they should all be classified the same.

More generally, many MAJCOM and Air Force headquarters-level organizations, FOAs, and DRUs are classifiable at the ORG kind–type level (typically as

---

[5] The PAS-implied hierarchy may be less accurate for some activities outside the Air Force, such as those related to joint service organizations, but such activities are likely to be classified as continuing missions, regardless of their true hierarchy.

[6] That is, support that is not closely linked to a combat unit, that does not represent a continuing mission, and is not involved in base operation. Some civil engineering units and military bands are examples.

[7] This section focuses on MDS authorizations that are used as input to BIM; therefore, it excludes MDS authorizations of ARC civilian technicians, CMEs, and other positions described in Appendix D.

Table 3.1

**Classification of Some MDS
Authorizations as Continuing
Missions Based on ORG Type**

ORG Type	Title
ag	Agency
bd	Band
bl	Battle lab
ce	Center
cl	College
cm	Command
du	Direct reporting unit
fe	Federal agency
fo	Field operating agency
gd	Guard
hq	Headquarters
hs	HQ USAF support
me	Med
sa	Separate operating agency
sr	Service

Table 3.2

Approach Used for the BIM Classification of MDS Authorizations

Level at Which BIM Category Is Set	Possible Combinations	Combinations Already Classified	Combinations Currently Classified	Related MDS Authorizations
ORG type	59	0	50	102,540
ORG kind and type	792	452	251[a]	121,993
ORG kind and type and CMD	1,196	814	275	205,164
PAS	10,136	8,277	1,859	203,968
PAS and FAC	40,739	40,739	0	0
MDS[b] total			2,837	633,665

[a]The full listing of the ORG kinds and types that determine a unit's BIM classification is given in Table B.1 (Appendix B).

[b]June 2000 MDS for fourth quarter FY 2001 found in the BIM input file (AFMRF, 2001a).

"Continuing Mission"). In fact, of the 792 different pairs of organization kind and type we found in the MDS, 703 (452 plus 251) are homogeneous enough to fall into a single BIM category. These 703 cover 224,533 MDS authorizations (102,540 plus 121,993), more than a third of the total of 633,665. The remaining 89 need to be disaggregated to permit classification. Even so, simply breaking them down by MAJCOM (into 382 kind–type–MAJCOM elements) settled the classification of another 205,164 MDS authorizations in 275 kind–type–MAJCOM elements.

The remaining 107 (382 minus 275) such elements required further disaggregation to the PAS level. For example, fighter squadrons (ORG kind "ftr," type "sq") in AETC were all assigned to the continuing mission BIM category, because their mission is training. For fighter squadrons outside AETC, we had to go to the PAS level, because, while most are deployable forces, there are a few training units and in-place forces among them. While the model permits disaggregation of PAS codes to the four-character FAC level, we did not find it necessary for the initial runs presented in this document. Thus, all 633,665 authorizations in the MDS could be assigned to BIM categories by reviewing 2,837 units or aggregates thereof.

Assigning TPFDD Demands to BIM Categories

Background on UTCs and TPFDDs. The elemental unit for manpower deployment planning is the UTC package (HQ USAF, 1998), which is identified by a five-character alphanumeric code. Each UTC is postured by one of the MAJCOMs, and, therefore, its associated component (active, Reserve, or Guard) is known. If the UTC requires manpower,[8] its composition is specified in a manpower force packaging (MANFOR) data table, which must be formally approved (HQ USAF, 1999a) before it becomes part of the Air Force–Wide UTC Availability System (AFWUS), the inventory of all approved UTCs. The MANFOR details each person's desired capability down to the AFSC, FAC, and officer grade or enlisted skill level. Each aviation UTC's description field also specifies the associated type and number of aircraft. Note that aviation UTCs begin with the numeral 3; see Table 3.3. For aggregate two-character UTC categories, see Table 3.4. The UTC table also provides transportation details (not directly relevant to manpower requirements), such as number of passengers.

An Air Force TPFDD[9] states deployment manpower and equipment tailored to meet a specific contingency. The manpower requirements are specified as a list of UTC packages that normally need to deploy,[10] although some stay in place. When a TPFDD file has MANFOR position information, it is said to have level-4 detail (level-2 detail if given at the UTC level). The TPFDD also provides details on the tasked unit sourcing the UTC, aerial ports of debarkation (APODs), aerial ports of embarkation (APOEs), required due dates, etc.

---

[8] Some UTCs involve no manpower, only equipment and its corresponding transportation information.

[9] For a description of TPFDD topics, see HQ USAF (1998).

[10] The ULN field can be used to track multiple instances of the same UTC.

Table 3.3

Aggregate One-Character UTC Categories

UTC First Character[a]	Functional Area
0	Infantry
1	Artillery, air defense missiles, space
2	Armor, antitank, tracked vehicles
3	Aviation flight units, mission aircraft
4	Engineer, topographic service
5	Warships, craft administration, aviation training
6	Communications, communications maintenance, electronics, signals
7	Tactical control, weather, rescue, command and control
8	Unconventional warfare, Navy mobile units, aviation
9	Miscellaneous combat, combat support, and combat service support
A	Task organization
B	Brigade service support
C	Command headquarters, DoD agencies
D	Defense and civilian government entities
E	Electronics
F	Medical, dental
G	Chemical, ordnance
H	Maintenance and ship development, construction, and maintenance
J	Supply, supply support services
K	Research, development, test, and evaluation
L	Administration, postal, courier, morale, mortuary affairs
M	Flight auxiliary and administration
N	Aviation support maintenance
P	Intelligence, counter intelligence
Q	Military police, security, law enforcement
R	Personnel, administration, information, reserve forces
S	Finance, comptroller, audit, contracts procurement
T	Training
U	Transportation and cargo handling, motor
V	Civil affairs, military assistance
W	Aircraft development
X	Posts, camps, rescue, weather, stations, base
Y	Naval support elements
Z	Miscellaneous

[a]The Joint Staff does not permit the use of the letters *I* and *O* as UTC designators.

A UTC may be *sourced* to a unit identified with a UIC (a part of the PAS code): A specific unit may be tasked to provide a person that has the desired capability.[11] Not all TPFDD demands, however, may be sourced.

---

[11] Sometimes a sourced UTC is fragmented, i.e., portions of one UTC are to be supplied by different units, possibly from different MAJCOMs.

Table 3.4

Aggregate Two-Character Categories for Miscellaneous UTCs

UTC	UTC2	Force Type	Unit Type Description
3AZ99	3A	TSS	Support
3BZ99	3B	SBS	Bombardment
3CZ99	3C	ACC	Airborne command and control communications
3DZ99	3D	TEW	Tactical electronic warfare–intelligence
3EZ99	3E	ADI	Fighter interceptor
3FZ99	3F	TFS	Fighter squadron
3MZ99	3M	AES	Aeromedivac
3NZ99	3N	TAS	Airlift
3RZ99	3R	TRS	Reconnaissance
3SZ99	3S	SOF	Special operations
3TZ99	3T	ARR	Air rescue and recovery
3WZ99	3W	WEA	Weather
3YZ99	3Y	ARS	Air refueling
4FZ99	4F	CES	Engineering
6ZZ99	6Z	CSS	Communications, computers, postal, information management
9AZ99	9A	HQS	Headquarters
CZZ99	CZ	CMD	JMA augmentation
FFZ99	FF	MED	Medical
HFZ99	HF	MNT	Maintenance
HHZ99	HH	MMS	Munitions
ISZ99	IS	ADI	Air defense
JFZ99	JF	SUP	Supply, fuels
PZZ99	PZ	INT	Intelligence
QFZ99	QF	SPS	Security forces, Office of Special Investigations
RAZ99	RA	ADM	Information management
RFZ99	RF	PER	Personnel
TEZ99	TE	ACE	Airlift control
TFZ99	TF	TCS	Tactical air control system
TFZ99	TF	TNG	Training
UFZ99	UF	TRN	Transportation
XFZ99	XF	SPT	Bare base support
XRZ99	XR	ARR	Rescue
XWZ99	XW	WEA	Weather

SOURCE: HQ USAF (1998), Figure 4.1.

Classification of Unit-Tasked TPFDD Manpower Demands. It is possible to assign a TPFDD's manpower positions to BIM categories when the TPFDD has manpower (level-4) details. Appendix C describes the pitfalls in generating this level of detail from a UTC-level TPFDD. Unfortunately, one still cannot count on fully accurate sourcing when getting Air Force TPFDDs with manpower position details. Given that fixing UTC sourcing is beyond the scope of our work, we proceeded with the manpower classification from the TPFDD data as received.

A sourced TPFDD with the manpower-position level of detail includes sufficient information (has UIC or PAS, AFSC, FAC) for our methodology to assign a position to a BIM category. The same criteria as for MDS authorizations apply. Problems in the resulting BIM classifications are mainly due to the input's inaccurate unit sourcing of positions. The discussion below presents shortcuts that can identify approximate BIM categories for mistasked TPFDD positions.

For example, a UTC in a TPFDD often calls for resources that are not actually in the unit tasked in the TPFDD. This is especially so for aviation UTCs: Although the tasked unit (UIC) can provide many of an aviation UTC's resources, some of that UTC's resources may have to come from another unit (e.g., a supply squadron) not explicitly tasked. Unless the UIC for this TPFDD requirement is changed to the actual unit with the resources, the BIM category, inferred from the nominal UIC tasking, may not be correct.

According to our analyses of the TFA TPFDD, such mistasking in the TPFDD data leads to two main problems. The first occurs when some of the resources in an aviation UTC tasked to a deployable forces UIC are available only in different UICs classified as in-place support. The second occurs when an aviation or maintenance UTC is tasked to the wing headquarters UIC (usually classified as in-place support) instead of to the aviation or maintenance units in that wing.

We examined the TPFDD aviation and maintenance UTCs to determine which of the FACs within them could usually be found in aviation and maintenance units, as opposed to units that we would normally classify as in-place support. We used this examination to establish a set of rules for determining the BIM classification for a TPFDD demand (from aviation and maintenance UTCs) using the FACs for the resources in these UTCs. For example, certain FACs pertain to aircrews and to aircraft maintenance personnel, and these FACs are found almost exclusively in aviation and maintenance units (deployable forces); FACs that pertain to supply functions are found almost exclusively in supply squadrons (in-place forces); and FACs that pertain to command and operations staff functions are found mostly in wing headquarters or operations group headquarters units (in-place forces).

These tentative rules help us understand the nature of the problem and could help to correct the BIM category classification for the kinds of problem conditions that we observed most often in TFA-I data. For the assessments in Section 4, we chose not to use these rules, in part because there is still one unhandled potential problem that arises when a TPFDD has aviation or maintenance UTCs incorrectly tasked to a support unit (usually to a wing headquarters) when they should have been tasked to units we would have classified as in-place forces. There is probably no substitute for thoroughly checking the tasking of aviation and maintenance UTCs and correcting cases of mistasking to support units.

Classification of Unsourced TPFDD Demands. In principle, it is possible to handle unsourced TPFDD demands using the UTC's leading characters[12] and the FAC to infer whether to classify the UTC's manpower requirements as deployable forces or support. As noted earlier, the TFA TPFDD lists unsourced demands for 9,329 positions, most in support (see table A.2). Therefore, as a first-order approximation, we classified them as active component support.

Highlight 2: Estimating the In-Place Support Requirements

A BIM estimates the in-place support requirements. This discussion largely refers to RAND's modified version of BIM (BIM-R).

As Figure 3.1 shows, BIM operates on the MDS authorizations that are classified as support. BIM adjusts this input to account for the base's change in workload in implementing the TPFDD for the scenario considered, as well as the longer workweek in effect for scenarios that include at least one MTW.

TFA-I's BIM produced only whole numbers for manpower positions, because of manual intervention. BIM-R, however, may produce fractional positions, which we consider acceptable for generating an aggregate measure of requirements.

The main elements of both versions of BIM are as follows:

- Model logic and output:
  — making support adjustments to account for workload changes[13] and wartime's longer workweek to produce in-place support requirements
- Main model inputs:
  — MDS authorizations classified as support.
  — the number of deployers by base and component (active, Reserve, Guard)
- Parameters to model logic:[14]

---

[12] The unit type code follows a JCS-established naming convention in which the first UTC character classifies UTCs according to previously defined categories (see Table 3.3).

[13] Including those resulting from the departure of deployers.

[14] We refer to data inputs that affect a model's relationships among variables as *parameters*.

— peacetime and wartime manpower availability factors (work hours per month)

— factors to arrive at new workload from the peacetime workload.

This subsection discusses the various adjustments BIM makes and the basis for assigning values to them. We conclude with one important adjustment made outside BIM-R: the exclusion of base operating support for unneeded deploying forces (the triangle in Figures 3.1 and 3.3).

BIM-R's Support Adjustment Logic

As noted in Figure 3.1, deployed support in the TPFDD, including BOS for bare bases, automatically becomes part of the requirements and is not subject to the adjustments described in this subsection, which focuses on home-station in-place support.

BIM-R can adjust peacetime authorizations to account for wartime's longer workweek, changes in the base mission population supported, and other workload factors (such as those related to heightened security during wartime). We next describe the logic behind each of these adjustments, then discuss which factors or combinations thereof we actually used.

Adjustments for Wartime's Longer Workweek. The change to a wartime workweek causes an increase in *capacity per person*. This factor can be computed as the ratio of wartime over the peacetime manpower availability factors (W-MAF and P-MAF, respectively), which are BIM input parameters directly proportional to the respective workweek lengths.

A separate process (which we describe below) estimates the home-station wartime workload (in man-hours). Because of the increase in capacity, handling this workload requires fewer people in wartime than it would otherwise. The resulting number of people become the new wartime requirement for in-place support. Following the example that TFA-I set, BIM-R first fills this requirement with existing civilian positions, then with military positions.

Adjustments for Changes in Mission Population Supported. Quite apart from TFA-I's requirements determination, Air Force planners must estimate the effect on BOS manpower requirements as a matter of course whenever active-component personnel are added to or deleted from any base (a *mission population* change). Official guidance (HQ USAF, 1999c) requires the planners to obtain the adjustment by multiplying the mission population change by 8 percent and subtracting that from (or adding it to) BOS. The 8-percent factor normally applies to changes in active-component military personnel on a base with an active-component base host; 4 percent may be used for civilians and 2 percent for Reserve or Guard drill populations (consisting of part-timers), when warranted.

TFA-I's BIM and BIM-R both use variations of the above approach to arrive at the BOS adjustments. Both BIMs require as an input the number of each base's deployers (by component). TFA's overarching guidance (HQ USAF XPMR, 2000b) suggested using 8 percent as the parameter and making no distinction among active, Reserve, or Guard component positions. FAMs, however, could override the guidance; it is not possible to tell from the BIM output data how often this factor was applied to the Reserve or Guard.

BIM-R applies the 8-percent parameter only to active-component deployers and makes no corresponding downward adjustment for deploying Air Reserve Component (ARC) tenants. We chose not to use the official adjustment factor (2 percent) for the ARC population changes on BOS requirements because the effect is small[15] and because proper modeling to deal with this case was not worth the effort.

One example of the possible complications would be an ARC unit that is indeed the primary provider of base support on a Guard- or Reserve-owned base. We could have allowed for an ARC host by setting the model up to recognize such cases and apply a different factor. For expediency in getting results, we decided to forgo any such adjustment. However, future refinements could improve on this approximation.

When the mission population changes substantially, e.g., by more than half of the total base population, the 8-percent factor may be too small. For an extreme case, only a skeleton BOS may be necessary to keep a base open; however, our models have so far not been designed to handle such cases.

On-call forces may require support at their home bases, at least while they are awaiting the "call." However, misidentification of on-call forces in a TPFDD is likely, given that the conventions used to identify on-call and in-place units may vary even within a single TPFDD (see Appendix C). Depending on the assumptions used in trying to identify them, the on-call can be quite large,[16] which could have a large influence on estimates of required support.

---

[15] Most ARC base-support-type units are intended only to serve as wartime resources and do not provide much peacetime support.

[16] The TFA TPFDD may consider as many as eight FWEs to be on call; see Section 4.

If on-call forces are treated as deployers for in-place support calculations, their home bases will likely need fewer support positions; if these "on-call" forces are a way to label forces not needed in a scenario, they should be treated as such and be given visibility, because other adjustments to requirements for unused forces may be necessary. Clearly, the most demanding situation is considering a large segment of the forces to be on call (e.g., eight FWEs) and also requiring support for them at their home base. Making support estimates that are more accurate will require defining on-call forces more precisely.

Additional Adjustments via a Workload Adjustment Factor. An additional workload adjustment input to BIM-R allows effects other than changes in the mission population supported. For example, more security posts may be necessary to guard a base in wartime. TFA-I's BIM also accepted a level-of-service factor as an input (parameter), which results in a change of workload; however, this type of adjustment appears to have been used rarely. In BIM-R, the 8-percent adjustment for deployers and this additional workload factor, are together deemed sufficient to represent workload changes.

Workload factors for the Reserve and Guard are another issue. A more-thorough examination of how to handle ARC support units may find that some units have no wartime in-garrison support function. BIM's workload adjustment factor should be set to zero for such units. We did not, however, do this in our analysis.

Selection of BIM Adjustment Methods and Corresponding Data

BIM-R provides three alternative methods for adjusting MDS support authorizations. Exactly one of these methods must be chosen for positions in the BIM support category:

- Apply only the workload adjustment factor described just above. (If this factor is set to 1.0 and if there are no other changes, the MDS authorization is effectively straightlined to become part of the requirements.)

- Apply only the adjustments for changed workload and for wartime's longer workweek (i.e., W-MAFs). We refer to this as the MAF-only method.

- Apply the adjustments for changed workload, for wartime's longer workweek, and for the change in mission population. We refer to this as the 8-percent-plus-MAF method.

BIM-R allows any nonnegative number to be the workload factor. Since we had no basis for making a different choice, we set the workload adjustment factor to

1.0 for all demonstration cases described in this document. For the current implementation of BIM-R, the different BIM methods can be applied only based on the organizational unit (via PAS, ORG number, kind, type, MAJCOM, etc.) and FAC. This means that, for a given unit and FAC, all support positions would use the same adjustment method. For the demonstrations we describe in this report, we applied the same adjustment method to all FACs within a unit, except for a few cases in which the adjustment methods depended on the FAC.

Figure 3.4 shows the actual profile of the support-adjustment methods we selected. For the active component, we selected the MAF-only method for about 55 percent of the support authorizations and the 8-percent-plus-MAF method for most of the remainder (a few were straightlined). For example, civil engineering squadrons usually used the MAF-only adjustment, because the workloads for civil engineering functions (consisting of building and ground maintenance and firefighting, among others) are usually unaffected by changes in base population.

We used the MAF-only adjustment method for support authorizations in the Reserve and Guard (no 8-percent or similar factor, as noted earlier).

Source of MAF Parameter Data for BIM

We have discussed how we assigned adjustment values based on population-supported (8 percent or 0 percent) and workload adjustment factors (1.0). That leaves the workweek factor, which is related to the MAFs. For the active

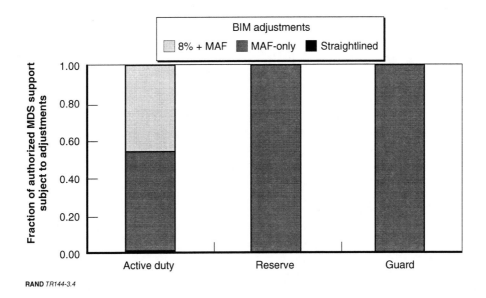

RAND TR144-3.4

**Figure 3.4—Profile of Our Actual Selection of
BIM-R Support-Adjustment Methods**

component, we used standard Air Force peacetime and wartime full-time MAFs for military, U.S. civilian, and foreign hires.[17] TFA-I did not treat the special case of part-timers. We judged the peacetime MAF factors to be inappropriate for the Reserve and Guard because both have many part-time or drill authorizations. Part-timers clearly have a shorter average workweek in peacetime. In peacetime, drilling members of the Reserve and Guard work at least 12 weekends plus 2 weeks per year. However, some ARC personnel, such as aircrews, drill at higher rates than is typical for others. We estimate that active-duty personnel (who work full time) participate from 210 to 220 days per year (excluding annual leave and holidays); ARC drill members participate at least 38 days per year (which is close to 18 percent of what full-timers put in). Therefore, lacking historical drill workweek data and given that the ARC has some full-timers, we made an approximation that both Reserve and Guard full-time and drill military personnel combined have a peacetime workweek that is only 25 percent of that of active-component personnel. This coarse estimate can be revised when better estimates become available.

As Figure 3.5 shows, the adjustment for part-timers has a major effect on the estimates of manpower for Reserve and Guard in-place support. The light gray bars show the total number of MDS authorizations for in-place support, military and civilian, in each reserve component. First, assume that all Reserve and Guard authorizations are full-timers. Then, because the workweek length changes from full-time peacetime (nominally 40 hours per week) to the corresponding wartime (nominally 60 hours per week), the number of people required to handle the workload in wartime is only about two-thirds of that in peacetime (see the adjacent bar in the figure).

But not all Reserve and Guard are full-timers (although civilians are). Therefore, with our assumed peacetime average military workweek of 25 percent of the full-time workweek (full-time and part-time personnel combined), it takes even fewer people to handle the military workload, which we assume to be constant (see the dark gray bar in Figure 3.5). The adjustment for part-timers reduces the Guard requirement, for example, from 33,000 to 10,000.

Support Adjustments Due to Unused Deployable Forces

Because TFA-I assumed that all forces (both deployable and in-place) were required for the two-MTW scenario, it did not have to address the issue of how

---

[17] In BIM-R, we set the MAF for foreign hires to be the same as for U.S. civilians. The discrepancy between the two factors is small and, in our view, did not warrant special handling in the model.

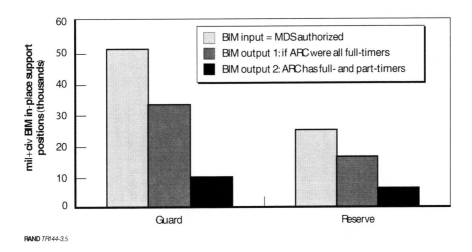

RAND *TR144-3.5*

**Figure 3.5—Sensitivity to Peacetime Workweek in Estimating
Guard and Reserve In-Place Support Manpower**

to handle forces a scenario did not explicitly use. We cannot, in general, make that assumption for smaller scenarios.

As noted earlier, documentation is needed about any new or existing policy that specifies the retention of additional forces for other purposes. We provided one theoretical example of this earlier: the overseas forward-presence policy that would retain forces in USAFE and PACAF.

If the Air Force selects a requirements policy that substantially changes the force structure, the methodology would need to be different from the one we propose below. When substantial changes are made to the infrastructure, this methodology misses, for example, adjustments that would be necessary for the wholesale logistics (depots) or the training infrastructure.

There are two steps for adjusting BOS for unused forces: First, determine the deployable forces not used; second, determine the BOS that is consequently not needed. To determine the deployable forces a given scenario does not use, we must match TPFDD units, MDS authorizations, and the aircraft inventory (HQ USAF XPPE, 2001) to find what is in the MDS but not either in the TPFDD or among the designated in-place forces. For example, if the Air Force's total primary aircraft authorization (PAA) exceeded a particular scenario's deployable requirements by 72 active-component fighters, 30 Reserve fighters, and 45 Guard fighters, we would label as unused the forces and the corresponding wartime, in-place support for one generic active-component fighter wing, two Reserve fighter wings, and three Guard fighter wings (assuming that generic active-component fighter wings have 72 aircraft and that the Reserve and Guard fighter wings have 15 aircraft).

Suppose an entire wing of forces and support are unused. There are two ways to arrive at the proper in-place support. The first alternative is to remove the actual support for the unused wing (including its base opening package) from the input to BIM, so that no requirements for this wing appear in the in-place support rectangle on the requirements column (right side of Figure 3.1). We do not use this approach because it identifies a specific base to eliminate.

The second alternative is a logically equivalent approach that uses generic wings. First note that, by definition, an unused wing has no deployers. Here, consistent with Figure 3.1, the actual wing's support is not excluded from the BIM input. Therefore, the BIM output includes this wing's in-place support after making adjustments for changing MAFs. In this approach, we remove from the BIM output the BIM-adjusted in-place support of a generic wing (not the actual unused wing); this is the dark triangle in Figure 3.1. A separate BIM run estimates the amount of support to be removed by using as the input the support (including its base opening package) of the generic wing for same aircraft type and component.

The second approach, which we prefer, requires defining generic active, Reserve, and Guard wing structures for particular types of aircraft (F-15 wings, A-10 wings, C-130 wings, KC-135 wings, etc.). This creates a level playing field for comparing requirements for different scenarios and avoids choosing specific bases to eliminate under a specific scenario.

This approach also allows us to deal with multiple partial wings of the same type that are unused. If the equivalent of two and a half wings are unused (rough aggregation is all right), we can delete the in-place support (BIM output) for the two generic wings and redistribute the remaining half-wing among the wings that are used (we prefer not to try to delete a fraction of a wing because additional assumptions would be required regarding base opening packages).

4. Manpower Requirements for Sample Alternative Scenarios

This section compares the implications on requirements of various policies and scenarios. To assess the ramifications of our departures from the TFA methodology, the section also compares our two-MTW results with those of TFA-I[1] and with MDS authorizations. We made such comparisons for active-component manpower, for the reserve components, and for the total force. We begin by defining scenarios.

Scenarios

There were four basic scenarios:

1. TFA-I's two-MTW scenario (AFMRF, 2001b)

2. a one-MTW scenario for southwest Asia (SWA), derived from scenario 1

3. a one-MTW scenario for northeast Asia (NEA), derived from scenario 1

4. a group of five simultaneous Dynamic Commitment vignettes (HQ USAF XPMR, 2001).

We then combined or elaborated on these scenarios in various ways. This section analyzes such scenarios and, to show their relative strengths, reports their associated fighter aircraft requirements (taken directly from the related documentation or inferred from the corresponding TPFDD) in FWEs.

The Basic Scenarios

The two-MTW scenario is that used in TFA-I. The vignettes represent a sampling of peacetime engagements or SSCs, including Operation Northern Watch (ONW) and Operation Southern Watch (OSW).[2]

---

[1] The results shown here for TFA-I are based on data received from the Air Force; in particular, they are based on version 3 of the TFA wartime file as received April 20, 2001 (AFMRF, 2001c), which includes Air Staff changes up to that date.

[2] ABTech, Inc. (now Alion Science and Technology) provided these vignettes to the Air Force; according to the Air Force, AF/XOC and JCS have also used them.

We derived the TPFDDs for the illustrative one-MTW scenarios from the TFA two-MTW TPFDD. The first two characters of the TFA TPFDD's unit line number (ULN) defined categories we used in deriving the sample one-MTW TPFDDs (see Table 4.1).

All TFA TPFDD demands identified as East were allocated to the SWA one-MTW TPFDD, and all those identified as West were allocated to the NEA TPFDD. In both the NEA and SWA TPFDDs, we included support requirements for three bare bases in theater (Fisher, 2000) and other unique requirements (SSCs, military operations other than war, and operational plans other than those for two MTWs that were not covered elsewhere).

The TFA TPFDD includes eight FWEs that could be intended to be on-call reinforcements or replacements for deployed MTW forces or to be reserves for undesignated, separate, pop-up contingencies that might occur simultaneously with the MTW. They are supplemented by sufficient BOS to operate out of collocated operating bases (COBs), i.e., collocated at bases already in use for other purposes. We apportioned the eight FWEs to SWA or NEA depending on their destination country.[3]

Because of their proximity to SWA, we assumed that all TPFDD demands in the group labeled "USAFE in support of two MTWs" (see Table 4.1) were allocated to SWA. However, the apportionment of the TPFDD demands in "CONUS in support of two MTWs" to SWA or NEA depended on the preponderant destination of the forces deploying from their home bases.

Table 4.1

**Allocation of TFA-I's Two-MTW TPFDD Demands
to Get One-MTW TPFDDs**

Two-MTW TPFDD Characterization (ULN Category)	1-MTW TPFDD	
	SWA	NEA
East	X	
West		X
8 FWEs	Split	
3 bare bases	X	X
Unique (common to all)	X	X
USAFE in support of 2 MTWs	X	
CONUS in support of 2 MTWs	Split	

---

[3] Their destination is given as "[country name]-UNKN," i.e., their intended base within the named country is unknown.

Comparing the Basic Scenarios

A first-order comparison of requirements at the FWE level will provide useful context for comparing our estimates of manpower requirements for some scenarios. The description fields of the UTCs for each scenario imply the number of FWEs for each, as shown in Figure 4.1. Not surprisingly, each one-MTW scenario requires roughly half the number of FWEs needed for two MTWs.

Unfortunately, the two-character ULN field prefix does not by itself allow the identification of swing forces.[4] Therefore, we did not adjust for swing forces in deriving the one-MTW scenarios. While this could lead to an underestimate of requirements, the error would be small because there are usually few swing forces. We would, for example, underestimate one-MTW requirements in NEA if a USAFE wing deployed to SWA were intended to swing to NEA once conflict got under way there in a two-MTW scenario.

Deriving and Comparing Combined and Conditioned Scenarios

The scenarios we considered included those indicated above, combinations of them (e.g., NEA plus vignettes), and simple or combined scenarios conditioned

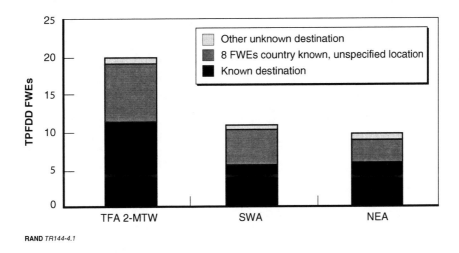

RAND TR144-4.1

**Figure 4.1—Allocation of Fighter Aircraft in TFA
Two-MTW TPFDD to Get One-MTW TPFDDs**

---

[4] Swing forces appear in the TPFDD at least twice, in the original and the subsequent deployment(s). The TFA two-MTW TPFDD that the Air Force (AFMRF, 2001b) provided reportedly contained only one instance of the swing forces. We did not verify this claim because the RDD field that helps in the identification had been removed.

by the theoretical requirements policies defined in Section 3. This report identifies the latter using one of the following suffixes:

- DEF—assumes that all deployable forces are treated as requirements (as did TFA-I), not just those in the TPFDD.
- FWD—assumes that all USAFE and PACAF deployable forces are treated as requirements, irrespective of their presence in the TPFDD.

Figure 4.2 shows the FWEs required for the two-MTW, SWA, vignette, and two "enhanced" NEA scenarios. Note that, in terms of FWEs, the vignettes approximate a one-MTW scenario. Because the vignettes already include ONW and OSW, it would lead to double counting if we combined them with the SWA one-MTW scenario. Instead, we combined the vignettes with NEA to get the scenario labeled "NEA+vign+FWD." In this first approximation, we did not attempt to identify or exclude conflicts in the taskings, e.g., if a unit is tasked for both NEA and the vignettes. The total FWEs for one MTW and the vignettes exceed 20 FWEs. That could indicate either double-tasking or that current forces are insufficient for one MTW and the vignettes combined. Determining which is the case would require more-thorough review and comparison of unit taskings than we were able to undertake here.

Summary of Scenarios

The following are the scenarios for which we report estimates of manpower requirements and our descriptors for them:

- 2-MTW—the requirements for TFA's two-MTW TPFDD (AFMRF, 2001b)

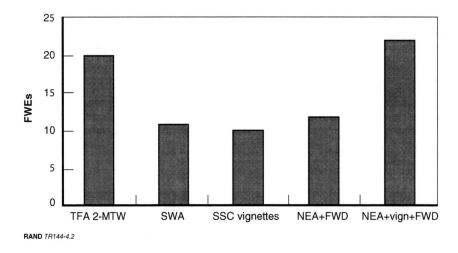

RAND TR144-4.2

Figure 4.2—TPFDD Fighter Aircraft for Alternative Scenarios

- 2-MTW+DEF—the requirements for TFA's two-MTW TPFDD and treating all deployable forces as required, irrespective of their presence in the TPFDD

- SWA—the requirements for the one-MTW SWA TPFDD, as derived from TFA's two-MTW TPFDD (Table 4.1)

- SWA+FWD—the requirements for the one-MTW SWA TPFDD, under the overseas forward presence policy

- NEA+vign+FWD—the requirements for the one-MTW NEA TPFDD combined with the Dynamic Commitment vignettes (SSCs), under the overseas forward presence policy

- TFA-I—TFA-I's requirements (AFMRF, 2001c), as computed by the Air Force.[5]

The manpower authorizations, labeled *MDS authorized,* are natural candidates for comparison against the requirements estimates for scenarios. For the MDS authorized data, we use the MDS for the fourth quarter of FY 2001 (MDS dated June 2000), which was also TFA-I's input file (AFMRF, 2001a).

Notes Applicable to Our Requirement Comparisons

With the exception of TFA-I and the MDS authorizations (which we did not compute), we used the approach we described in Section 3 to estimate requirements. However, we have not yet incorporated the downward in-place support slice adjustment for deployable forces not used in a scenario. We felt that it would be less confusing (for determining the cause of differences) not to include such adjustments when comparing the results for two-MTW scenarios. The results shown in this section therefore do not reflect such an adjustment and are therefore somewhat higher than they would be had it been made. Both the authorizations and requirements shown exclude some manpower categories (individual mobilization augmentees [IMAs], CMEs, students, etc.; see Appendix D) that require special handling.

Most results for the cases compared in this section (and Appendix A) are shown in terms of the four BIM categories. All the cases presented use the refined BIM classification from Section 3, except for the results of TFA-I, which use TFA-I's own slightly different classification (see Appendix B for a comparison of BIM classifications).

---

[5] This is also known as the *TFA wartime file.* The numbers reported here may not include a final set of subsequent manual adjustments that AF/XPMR and functional representatives made to both quantities and the assigned BIM categories.

Besides the four BIM categories shown in Figure 3.1, the results shown in this section further divide the support category into three parts (see also Figure 3.1):

1. in-place support—the adjusted BOS (see Section 3)
2. support deployed—the sourced TPFDD demands classified as support
3. support deployed unsourced—the unsourced TPFDD demands classified by default as active-component support.

Note that TFA's two-MTW TPFDD included 9,322 unsourced demands; the corresponding numbers for the one-MTW scenarios may be too small to be discerned in a given graph.

Military Requirements for the Active Component

The Effects of Policies Conditioning the Basic Scenarios

Figure 4.3 shows active-component military requirements for two basic scenarios and corresponding variations. The first two columns both show the manpower requirements for the basic two-MTW scenario, but the second column imposes the policy of treating all forces, deployable or in-place, as requirements. Naturally, 2-MTW+DEF requires more deployable positions. The last two columns in Figure 4.3 pertain to the one-MTW SWA scenario. The rightmost column imposes the policy that treats all PACAF and USAFE deployable forces as requirements, irrespective of their presence in the corresponding TPFDD.

These requirement policies make a noticeable difference. In the remainder of this section, we use the more-demanding variations, rather than the basic scenarios. It is unclear which scenarios may be officially adopted as being representative of scenarios below two MTWs, and we want to be generous with respect to the forces potentially viewed as requirements.

Because our manpower requirements include AFSC specialties, they are easy to summarize for selected specialties or career fields. Appendix A provides the results for some selected specialties in the context of looking for opportunities for improvements of the TFA-I methodology.

Comparison of Requirements for Different Scenarios and Methodologies

For the active component, Figure 4.4 compares computed military requirements to MDS authorizations and TFA-I's requirements. Comparing the first two

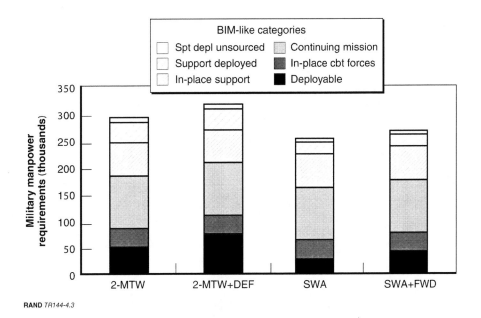

RAND *TR144-4.3*

**Figure 4.3—Active-Component Military Requirements
for Alternative Requirements Policies**

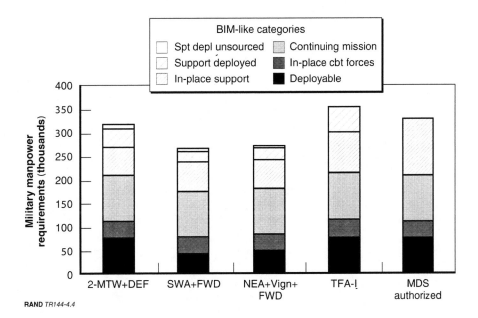

RAND *TR144-4.4*

**Figure 4.4—Active-Component Military
Requirements for Alternative Scenarios**

columns shows that the requirements for the two-MTW scenario exceed those for
one MTW by more than 50,000 positions in deployable forces and deployed
support.

However, they fall within the total MDS authorizations for the fourth quarter of FY 2001. Note that TFA-I's estimated two-MTW requirements exceed the MDS authorizations: The major discrepancy occurs in the support categories, all other categories being in close agreement. Differences between the TFA-I and 2-MTW+DEF requirements were also mainly in support. Appendix A, while focusing on specific career fields, points out that the discrepancy is consistent with some potential pitfalls predicted (from first principles) for the deployed support merge that produces the "wartime file" TFA-I requirements. One comparison from Figure 4.4 is curious. The second and third columns in the figure differ by only about 6,000 positions, even though the second column is for one MTW and the third column uses about the same FWEs as the two-MTW scenario (see Figure 4.2). We expected to find a larger difference between the requirements of these scenarios, since one has approximately twice the FWEs of the other. To understand this, let us compare the TPFDD manpower (key input to the requirements-estimation methodology) for the one-MTW SWA scenario and for the SSC vignettes.

Figure 4.5 shows that the manpower demands for the SWA TPFDD and the SSC vignettes differ substantially, even though both scenarios require about the same number of FWEs (see Figure 4.2). Figure 4.6 compares the manpower per aircraft for these two scenarios. Again, the numbers for the vignettes are less than half than those for SWA. Clearly, the Air Force needs to reassess the suitability of these SSC vignettes for estimating Air Force requirements.

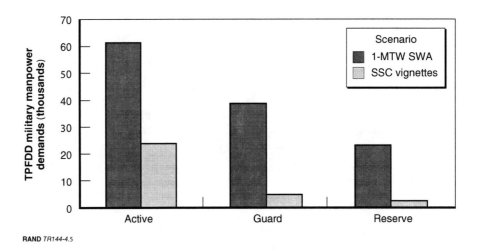

RAND TR144-4.5

**Figure 4.5—Military Demands in the SWA
One-MTW TPFDD and the SSC Vignettes**

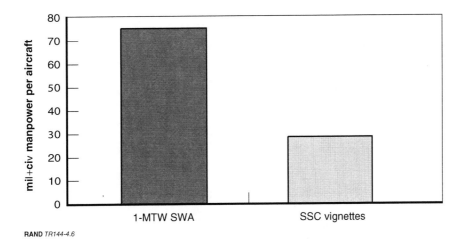

**Figure 4.6—Manpower per Aircraft in the SWA
One-MTW TPFDD and the SSC Vignettes**

Reserve and Guard Military Requirements

TFA-I results differ from our 2-MTW+DEF and from the MDS authorizations
more for the Reserve and Guard than for the active component; see Figure 4.7 for
the Reserve and Figure 4.8 for the Guard. For both components, our
2-MTW+DEF estimates and TFA's differ in the distribution of requirements
across BIM categories, and for the Guard, the totals differ greatly as well. The
TFA Guard requirement is also well short (by over 57,000 positions) of the MDS
authorizations. For the Reserve, the difference between TFA's method and ours
in the support BIM category reflects the differences in the classification of the
MDS authorizations (see Appendix B). For the Guard, the differences are larger
and not easily explained; it is conceivable that there were some unintentional
omissions in the TFA process. See Appendix A for an analysis of the TFA output
data.

We estimated that Reserve and Guard requirements for the 2-MTW+DEF
scenario are fewer than the MDS authorizations. The difference is small for the
Reserve but is about 16,000 positions for the Guard.

Total Force Requirements

Figures 4.9 and 4.10 show total manpower requirements across the active,
Reserve, and Guard components; Figure 4.9 excludes civilians, while Figure 4.10
includes them. As noted earlier, these results exclude IMAs and CMEs.

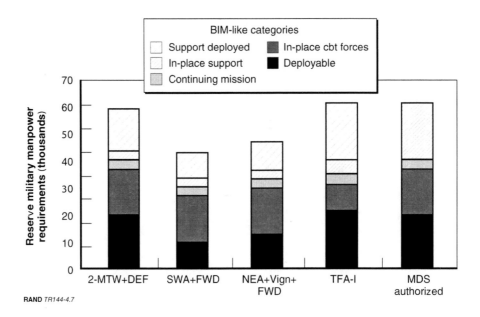

Figure 4.7—Reserve Military Requirements for Alternative Scenarios

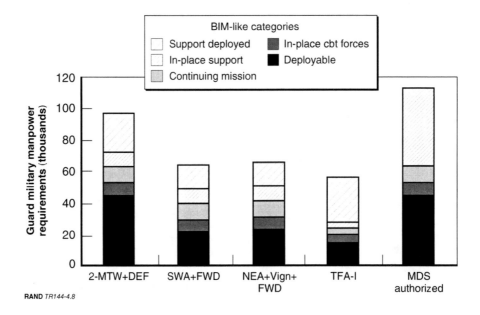

Figure 4.8—Guard Military Requirements for Alternative Scenarios

Additional Adjustments to Requirements

As we noted earlier in this section, we have not yet adjusted the requirement results downward for the support slice exclusion corresponding to deployable

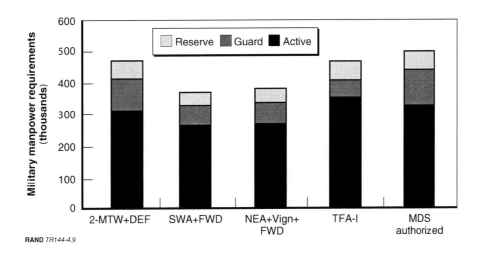

RAND TR144-4.9

Figure 4.9—Total Force Military Requirements for Alternative Scenarios

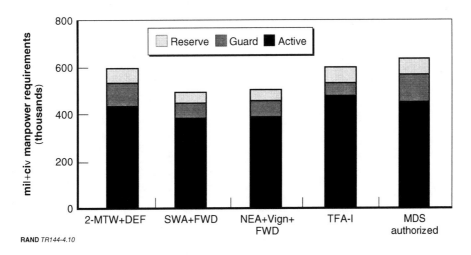

RAND TR144-4.10

**Figure 4.10—Total Force Military and Civilian
Requirements for Alternative Scenarios**

forces not used in a given scenario (if there are any). Clearly, these adjustments must still be made.

Air Force requirements estimates become inputs to other planning processes. The requirements computed here may also need to be folded in with positions for IMAs, CMEs, students, and others (see Appendix D). Some of the steps to fold these in are straightforward, and some use standard Air Force factors. We do not cover those topics here.

5. Adequacy of the Estimated Requirements for Peacetime Engagements

In Section 4, we examined various potential requirement policies, each of which involved at least one MTW and thus, we assumed, a general call-up of the reserve components. Here, to address another important issue, we depart from that assumption of call-ups to focus on the more commonly prevailing scenario of peacetime engagements or SSCs. In particular, we explore manpower issues related to the Air Force's organization for peacetime or SSC deployment, which follows EAF concepts (HQ USAF, 1999b). We review EAF manpower policies and assumptions and then assess the adequacy of manpower authorizations for meeting past EAF needs.

In the EAF original concept of operations, it was assumed that, as personnel deploy from a base for a given 90-day AEF rotation, the base and its remaining forces can accommodate the remaining home-station workload, perhaps by working extended hours. This section touches on this topic only lightly—only from a modeling perspective. A more in-depth look at this topic is necessary.

This section does not directly estimate peacetime or AEF requirements. Instead, in keeping with a capabilities-based view of the Air Force, we investigate whether the Air Force has adequate manpower resources for meeting peacetime SCC demands.

Our preliminary analysis found that the authorizations appear to be adequate. We close this section by highlighting potential problems that may help explain some of the stress apparently felt under the EAF implementation.

The Air Force in the EAF Environment

Peacetime SSCs with No Call-Up of Reservists

As of 2001, Air Force manpower requirements were sized to fight two MTWs, assuming full mobilization of the Reserve and Guard. However, under peacetime conditions, manpower requirements for peacetime engagements or SSCs are scheduled and met with *volunteer* participation of reservists and guardsmen (no call-up), while operating under the EAF environment.

That raises an important question: Are manpower positions that are sized to meet 2-MTW-based requirements (with full Reserve and Guard call-up) also sufficient to meet the peacetime engagement demands with no call-ups? We address this question next.

Rotations in the EAF Environment

The Air Force has organized itself to follow an EAF concept of operations, organizing the forces into ten rotational AEFs; two alternating, on-call, crisis-response AEWs;[1] and a group of enabler forces that includes special operations forces (SOF), global reach laydown, humanitarian relief operation, and low-density, high-demand forces (see Figure 5.1).

Each of the five pairs of rotational AEFs is scheduled to cover a 90-day period for possible deployment. Therefore, without overlap, the ten AEFs cover a 15-month cycle.[2]

The AEF 90-day rotational duration is consistent with an EAF's objective to restrict all deployment tour lengths and on-call periods to 90 days per 15-month cycle, thus allowing individuals to take some further TDY for other purposes and still not exceed the service's TDY objective. This Air Force objective is to keep

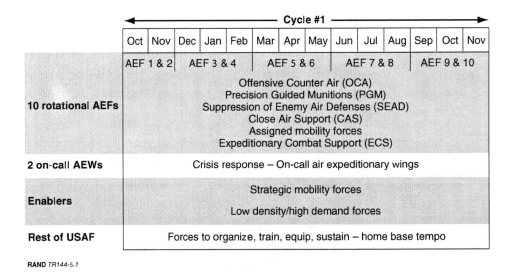

RAND TR144-5.1

Figure 5.1—Overview of the EAF Structure

---

[1] Beginning in cycle 4, the AEW forces are redistributed elsewhere in the EAF as the AEW concept is eliminated.

[2] As Figure 5.1 shows, the first rotation of cycle 1 lasted two months instead of three.

active duty personnel tempo at or below 120 days of temporary duty (TDY) per year (HQ USAF XOPE, 2000). This includes TDY for training, exercises, and other purposes, in addition to contingency operations. The AEF schedules and implementation policies try to provide greater predictability for when an individual is "vulnerable" to be deployed for contingency operations.

Each of the AEWs, however, was on call for alternating 120-day periods (90-day for cycle 1). The units assigned to the enabling forces are essentially on call all the time. These longer on-call periods for the AEWs and the enabling forces could result in deployments exceeding the TDY objective for these elements of the force. Therefore, the Air Force has to balance manpower demands against the deployment period limit it has specified for individuals.

Reserve and Guard volunteers can serve a portion of an AEF's 90-day period. In the absence of volunteers serving longer periods, the comparable personnel tour length limit for the Reserve and Guard is 15 days per cycle. Thus, up to six 15-day Reserve and Guard rotations may be necessary to cover a 90-day AEF rotation.

Information from the AEF Center, at Langley AFB, Virginia, indicates that the Guard and Reserve aim to provide 25 percent of the AEF rotational requirements for aviation manpower. The corresponding goals for expeditionary combat support (ECS) were 10 percent for cycle 2 and 13 percent for cycle 3 (Peck, 2001).[3]

EAF Implications for Requirements

One of the selling points of the EAF concept was that it would require no additional manpower resources. This translates into the presumption that current authorizations are sufficient to meet EAF needs, implicitly accepting the possibility that certain base organizations or functional areas may need to extend their workweeks to meet remaining workloads.[4]

EAF deployments can be analyzed using the same modeling concepts we used earlier. As in the case of an MTW (see Sections 2 and 3), there are deployments in the categories of both forces and support. In this subsection, we focus on the manpower requirements at the home base.

---

[3] Cycle 3 began on March 1, 2002.

[4] The realization that the EAF may in fact require additional resources was accepted when AEF backfill manpower authorizations were included in the 2001 MDS. The backfill authorizations were offset by decreases in other peacetime authorizations.

Estimating any manpower shortfall under the EAF requires an explicit assumption about the workweek length. However, according to AFMIA, as of 2002 there was no Air Force–wide special policy on the home-base workweek length for estimating requirements under the EAF. Instead, each base commander can make the adjustments he or she deems necessary.

Support Requirements

Support requirements need to include the support deployers and the in-place support at the home base. The latter could be estimated with a BIM, making downward adjustments to peacetime workload to account for the decrease in base mission population (the part of its deployable forces that actually deploys under the EAF) and to reflect a possible longer workweek during the AEF deployment. The BIMs do require, however, an explicit assumption about workweek length at the home station—which, lacking policy to the contrary—has to be assumed to be the standard peacetime workweek.

Deployable Force Requirements

Our manpower BIM classification assigns aircraft maintenance to the deployable forces category. But does this leave enough maintenance manpower at home to support the forces not deployed with the AEFs? Some argue that, when a squadron (or part of it) deploys to meet peacetime SSC demands, it takes more than a proportional share of the wing's maintenance and similar resources. Furthermore, deploying personnel with mid-level skills may leave insufficient resources for training personnel with lower-level skills. We do not address these issues in this document. We assume that the remaining maintenance resources can absorb any extra relative workload for the forces remaining at home through increases (of unspecified size) in their work hours.

Manpower Shortfalls and Backfill Issues

Being realistic about potentially high demands on a base requires thinking about the circumstances that could justify claims for home-station *backfill* requirements.

Providing extra manpower authorizations to every base affected by the AEFs would be expensive, especially since, by design, the changed workload on a given base is only temporary. Providing partial backfill manpower to a base does not eliminate the full shortfall. If some overall backfill authorizations were provided to the entire Air Force, they would have to be prorated to the bases having the actual constantly moving target. Unless the backfill constantly moves to where it is needed, prorated backfill would cause some bases to have too much and others not enough manpower at any moment.

Analytic Approach for an EAF Manpower Assessment

In this subsection, we examine whether TFA's two-MTW requirements are sufficient to cover the EAF peacetime SSC deployment demands, within the tour length limits set by AEF policy. However, because we performed this analysis before the TFA requirements were available, we used authorizations in the AEF libraries (AFMRF, 2000a) in lieu of requirements.

We compared peacetime SSC demands against the AEF library resources to arrive at an assessment of the ability of the full force to cover such demands.

Manpower Demand and Historical Data

The component commands, in coordination with the AEF Center (among others), arrive at a statement of requirements or demand for each rotational AEF period. When tasked to specific units, these requirements become a deployment requirements manning document (DRMD).

Because the rotational EAF pairs do not have identical aviation resources, actual demands may vary from one rotation to the next. Even when identical aircraft types and numbers are involved, component command managers have discretion in how they run their businesses. To analyze this demand variability, RAND obtained, with AFMRF's help, historical or projected demand data for the 90-day rotational periods corresponding to AEFs 5, 6, 9, and 10 for cycle 1 and AEFs 1 through 4 for cycle 2 (AFMRF, 2000b; AEF Center, 2000b).

Available Manpower for AEFs

The peacetime deployment demands within an AEF rotation are met by using the manpower positions in the UTC packages listed in the AEF libraries, which are allocated to the AEFs, AEWs, and enablers. Each library is constructed starting from the AFWUS, the list of approved UTC packages. A UTC, such as one in wing ECS, may be spread across different AEF rotations. If so, we assume that its inclusion in the library is a sign that the 90-day per cycle on-call or deployment tour length limits (15 days for the ARC) can be met. For example, part of the UTC can cover one AEF 90-day period, and a different part of the

UTC can cover another.[5] However, because the library does not allocate the on-call AEWs and enabler forces to the ten rotational AEFs, there is no a priori guarantee that the AEWs and the enablers meet their respective rotational limits per cycle.

Assessment of Manpower Adequacy to Meet AEF Peacetime Demand

This subsection reports our preliminary findings. To summarize, there were, for the most part, sufficient *authorizations* in the AEF library for cycle 2 to meet the peacetime deployment requirements specified in the historical DRMD data without a reserve components call-up. This may not be surprising, given the totals. However, we also verified that authorizations were sufficient in most skill categories within the desired deployment tour length limits. Later, we will contrast actual personnel assignments with manpower authorizations and note the implications.

Adequacy Rankings of Manpower Authorizations

Because SSC peacetime deployment demands vary with the AEF rotation period, we used the *average* demand over the AEF 90-day periods indicated earlier. We also examined the *peak* demand, that is, the highest requirement, by specialty group, in any of the four periods for which we had data. The numeric data in Table 5.1 give the average demand for some enlisted specialty groups. (The profile for the AFSC groups shown is approximately representative of other AFSC groups that are not shown.) The rightmost column gives the demand across all skill levels, whereas the other columns highlight individual skills (or their likely pay grade).

Unless otherwise noted, the manpower positions account for the different tour length limits per 15-month cycle for active duty and the ARC. The notes to Table 5.1 indicate the adequacy of the AEF library manpower positions. Half the cells in the total column for the specialty groups shown are not tagged with a note, indicating that the average demand can be met with the AEF library resources (cycle 2) allocated to the ten rotational AEFs. Note *b* indicates that the average demand can be met by reaching into the part of the AEF library allocated to the

---

[5] In principle, it is easier for the AEF Center, in trying to meet the 90-day tour length limit, to track which whole UTCs are part of rotations than to track people within a UTC. It may be known, for example, that a base has sufficient manpower for three UTC instances, in which case no more than three will be requested from that base each cycle, to avoid exceeding the deployment limit.

Table 5.1
Peacetime Average SSC Demand and Sample
Adequacy Ranking of Manpower Authorizations

| | Enlisted Skill Level and Grade | | | | | |
AFSC3	Skill 3 E1–3	Skill 5 E4–5	Skill 7 E6–7	Skill 9 E8	Skill 0 E9	SSC Average Total
1A0 In-flight refueling		15.8	6.3	0.3		22.3
1A1 Flight engineering		37.0	29.3	0.3		66.5
1A2 Aircraft loadmaster	5.0[a]	59.5	27.3	0.3		92.0
1A3 Airborne communication systems		16.3[b]	1.8[b]			18.0[b]
1A4 Airborne battle management systems		29.3[b]	2.3[b]	1.5[b]		33.0[b]
1A5 Airborne mission systems		17.3[b]				17.3[b]
1C0 Airfield management and operations resource management	1.3	44.0	19.0			64.3
1C1 Air traffic control		27.3	34.3[b]	5.8[b]		67.3
1C2 Combat control						
1C3 Command and control		29.3	19.8	1.8[c]		50.8
1C4 Tactical air command and control	6.0[b]	11.5[b]	4.5[b]			22.0[b]
1C5 Aerospace control and warning systems		42.0[b]	6.5[b]	0.5[b]		49.0[b]
1C6 Space system operations						
1N0 Intelligence applications		56.0	19.3	0.5		75.8
1N1 Imagery analysis		8.8[b]	3.5[b]			12.3[b]
1N2 SIGINT products		2.5[b]	1.0[c]		1.0[d]	4.5[b]
1N3 Linguist	3.3[b]	11.3[b]	10.3[b]	1.0[b]		25.8[b]
1N4 SIGINT analysis		12.5[b]	7.3[b]			19.8[b]
1N5 Electronic SIGINT exploitation		11.0[b]	1.8[b]			12.8[b]
1N6 Electronic systems security assessment		0.8[b]				0.8[b]
1S0 Safety			9.8		0.3[d]	10.0
1T0 Survival, Evasion, Resistance, and Escape training		0.5	1.0			1.5
1T1 Aircrew life support	0.3	50.8	10.0	1.0	0.3[d]	62.3
1T2 Pararescue		9.3[b]	6.0[b]			15.3[b]
1W0 Weather		33.3	20.0			53.3

[a]Unless a numeric entry has a note to the contrary, the average demand falls within the resources available in two AEFs.

[b]Average demand is more than two AEFs but still within EAF.

[c]Average demand is within EAF but breaks 90/15 rule.

[d]Average demand exceeds two AEFs plus one AEW and enablers (EAF total available).

two on-call AEWs or enabler forces. This is not necessarily an indication of a problem, because needed resources may appear mostly in the enabling forces (as is the case for the demands to which note *b* applies in this figure, which are for specialties in AWACS units and other elements found only or primarily in the enabler forces).

Skill levels cannot readily be substituted for each other, however, so the cells to the left of the total column are of greater interest. In those, about half the demands also could be met within the AEFs. Where they could not be met within the AEFs, the tour length limits could have been exceeded in some cases.

Note *c* identifies the demands that can be met with the AEF library resources **only** if they are exempted from the 90-day limit. We identified these specialty and skill groups as those whose demands over 90 days were within the total number of positions in the 15-month AEF library but whose demand-days would exceed 90 days' prorated share of the library position-days. In computing position-days, we assumed that an active-component library position can generate only 90 position-days per rotation period and that a Reserve or Guard position can generate 15 position days.[6] Note *c* applies to only two of the cells in Table 5.2, each with one or two demands on average.

Finally, note *d* indicates those for which the peacetime SSC demand cannot be met within the AEF library. Again, there are only three cases of this type, each with an average demand less than one.[7]

Table 5.2 shows a comparable set of measures for the *peak* (not average) over the periods for which data were available for this analysis. As expected, fewer cells are labeled with note *a,* etc. But they hardly indicate major problems in manpower authorizations.

In cycle 2, some AEW UTCs may have been fenced and therefore not used in AEF rotation schedules, something we did not know at the time of this analysis and, therefore, did not consider. Similarly, in cycle 3, new UTC availability coding included in the AFWUS may be used to identify UTCs that are used only as a step of last resort (Hitz and Cohen, 2001).

---

[6] History shows that a Reserve or Guard person may volunteer for more than 15 days; the position-days estimated here are, therefore, conservative estimates.

[7] Note that the table shows only adequacies or shortfalls, not excesses. In some cases, a high-skill-level position could serve that (typically managerial) position in more than one specialty simultaneously. But the demand data do not tell us where such an individual in a (single) designated specialty could have been serving in more than one capacity (and thereby be able to cover the apparent shortfall in a related specialty).

Table 5.2
Peacetime Peak SSC Demand and Sample
Adequacy Ranking of Manpower Authorizations

| | Enlisted Skill Level and Grade | | | | | |
| | Skill 3 E1-3 | Skill 5 E4-5 | Skill 7 E6-7 | Skill 9 E8 | Skill 0 E9 | SSC Peak Total |
AFSC3						
1A0 In-flight refueling		33.0[a]	16.0	1.0		50.0
1A1 Flight engineering		77.0[b]	59.0[b]	1.0		137.0[b]
1A2 Aircraft loadmaster	11.0[b]	130.0[b]	69.0[b]	1.0		211.0[b]
1A3 Airborne communication systems		25.0[b]	3.0[b]			28.0[b]
1A4 Airborne battle management systems		42.0[c]	3.0[b]	2.0[c]		47.0[b]
1A5 Airborne mission systems		25.0[b]				25.0[b]
1C0 Airfield management and operations resource management	5.0	90.0[b]	42.0[b]			137.0[b]
1C1 Air traffic control	18.0[d]	90.0[c]	85.0[c]	13.0[c]		206.0[c]
1C2 Combat control						
1C3 Command and control	1.0[b]	74.0[c]	57.0[c]	6.0[d]		138.0[c]
1C4 Tactical air command and control	7.0[b]	15.0[b]	6.0[b]			28.0[b]
1C5 Aerospace control and warning systems		76.0[c]	13.0[b]	2.0[b]		91.0[b]
1C6 Space system operations						
1N0 Intelligence applications	7.0[b]	128.0[b]	53.0[b]	1.0		189.0[b]
1N1 Imagery analysis		16.0[b]	6.0[b]			22.0[b]
1N2 SIGINT products		4.0[b]	2.0[c]		2.0[d]	8.0[b]
1N3 Linguist	6.0[b]	27.0[c]	25.0[c]	2.0[c]		60.0[b]
1N4 SIGINT analysis		15.0[b]	10.0[b]			25.0[b]
1N5 Electronic SIGINT exploitation		15.0[b]	2.0[b]			17.0[b]
1N6 Electronic systems security assessment						
1S0 Safety			19.0[b]			19.0
1T0 Survival, Evasion, Resistance, and Escape training		1.0	3.0			4.0
1T1 Aircrew life support	1.0	81.0	21.0	2.0		105.0
1T2 Pararescue		18.0[b]	11.0[b]			29.0[b]
1W0 Weather		72.0[b]	46.0			118.0

[a]Unless a numeric entry has a note to the contrary, the peak demand falls within the resources available in two AEFs.

[b]Peak demand is more than two AEFs but still within EAF.

[c]Peak demand is within EAF but breaks 90/15 rule.

[e]Peak demand exceeds two AEFs plus one AEW and enablers (EAF total available).

Potential ARC Contribution: A Sample Check for Civil Engineers

We wanted to assess the ability of the available ARC manpower positions to handle the demand of a pair of rotational AEFs. For this, we examined the data to see what fraction of a period's DRMD demands the Reserve and Guard could meet, without the help of the active component. We did this to assess the reasonableness of the stated objective of the Reserve component's filling 10 percent (or some greater percentage) of ECS peacetime demand.[8] We did enforce the deployment tour length limits per cycle set by policy: 90 days for active and 15 days for Reserve and Guard. The demand data were taken from the DRMDs for rotational AEFs 1 and 2 in cycle 2.

First, as Figure 5.2 shows, we considered civil engineer *officer* AFSC positions (AFSCs in the grouping 032E*[9]). We considered three possible sources of manpower positions:

1. ARC positions in the AEF library (no information as to how many might be technicians)

2. ARC positions in the MDS authorizations excluding the military technicians

3. ARC positions in the MDS authorizations including the military technicians.

Of the 25 demands for the referred AEF pair, source 1 could cover 35 to 40 percent of the demand, source 2 could cover slightly more than 60 percent, and source 3 could cover 100 percent. By definition, part-time military technicians also have full-time civilian jobs. We considered sources 2 and 3 separately because using technicians to meet an AEF pair's demand would be more disruptive to the continuing readiness and training mission of the Reserve elements that remain at home on a base that provides deployers.

Figure 5.3 presents a comparable analysis for civil engineering fire protection (enlisted AFSCs 3E7*). In this case, more than 30 percent of the peacetime demand could be met from the ARC AEF library alone, and more than 40 percent of the 241 positions could be met from all MDS Reserve and Guard authorizations.

Figure 5.4 presents another analysis, this one for CE Explosive Ordnance Disposal (enlisted AFSCs 3E8*). Overall, Figures 5.2 through 5.4 show that the relative potential contribution of the Reserve and Guard varies by AFSC group.

---

[8] AEF cycle 2.

[9] An asterisk acts as a "wild card" character to indicate that 0 or more additional characters may be part of the AFSC.

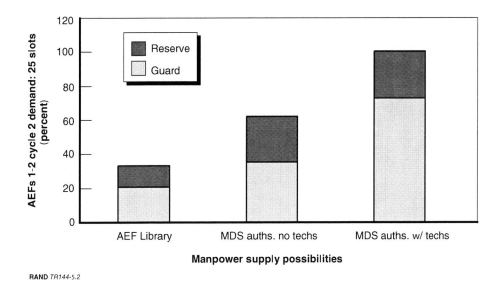

RAND *TR144-5.2*

Figure 5.2—Fill Rate for Civil Engineer Demands: Officer AFS 032E*

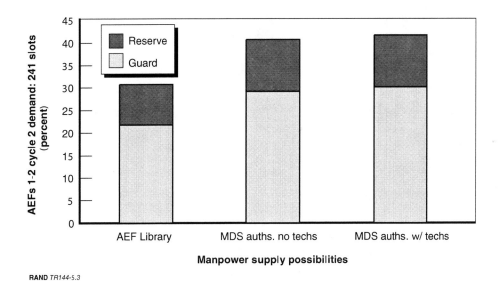

RAND *TR144-5.3*

Figure 5.3—Fill Rate for Civil Engineer Demands: Enlisted AFS 3E7*

In at least some cases, the ARC could meet the peacetime SSC demand without any active-component participation.

This particular look at civil engineers does not reflect volunteer rates. These rates are critical because, under current EAF policy, the Reserve and Guard volunteer for peacetime engagements. With this caveat, we note that Figures 5.2 and 5.3—but not 5.4—show that Reserve and Guard could cover up to three times the 10 percent of the demand that they set out to cover in cycle 2. Nevertheless, given

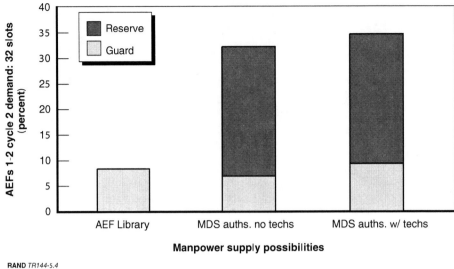

RAND TR144-5.4

Figure 5.4—Fill Rate for Civil Engineer Demands: Enlisted AFS 3E8*

that active-component manpower is the main source covering peacetime SSC demand, these results may indicate that existing authorizations are adequate for the AEF.

Factors That Affect the Availability of Individuals in the AEFs

Posturing More Positions in UTCs, AFWUS, and AEF Libraries

As Figures 5.2 through 5.4 showed for civil engineering, a substantial portion of the Reserve and Guard for these AFSCs was not part of the AEF libraries in cycle 2. This was more pronounced for the active component (see Figure 5.5). A large block of active authorizations was not identified as deployable, as indicated by their absence from the AFWUS (AFMRF, 2002).

A "Corona Tasker"[10] triggered a 2001–2003 Air Force effort to posture additional positions in AFWUS UTCs. Because most of the AFWUS at the time was also part of the AEF library for cycle 2 (see Figure 5.6), posturing more UTCs could make more manpower resources available to AEF schedulers.

---

[10] This is an action item emanating from one of the "Corona" conclaves involving all four-star Air Force generals.

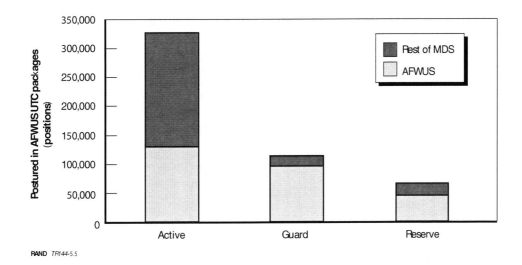

RAND *TR144-5.5*

Figure 5.5—Manpower Postured in the AFWUS (cycle 2)

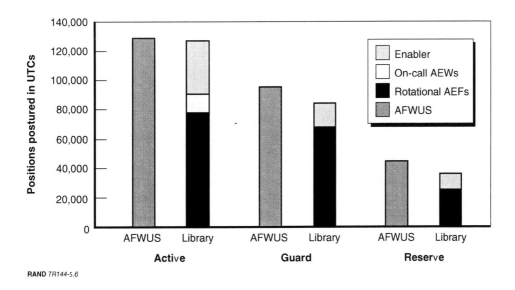

RAND *TR144-5.6*

Figure 5.6—Manpower Postured in AEF Libraries Versus the AFWUS (cycle 2)

AEF Participation of the Reserve and Guard

As noted earlier, the Reserve and Guard planned to meet 25 percent of the aviation and 10 percent (cycle 2) of the ECS AEF requirements. But some conditions limit the ARC's participation in the AEFs, e.g., lack of required skills and some requirements for tour lengths longer than 30 days, as established by the (theater) components (AEF Center, 2000a). In cycle 3, the ARC increased its participation to meet a goal of 13 percent of the ECS requirements.

62

Authorized Manpower Versus Personnel Assignments

Our assessment of the adequacy of current authorizations against peacetime SSC demands did not account for actual personnel assignments. To perform a preliminary examination of the differences between authorizations and assignments, we downloaded assigned personnel data from an Air Force Web site (HQ AFPC DPSA, 2000).

As Figures 5.7 through 5.8 show, assignments fall substantially short of the authorizations, especially in the middle grades. Consequently, if our calculations used assignments instead of authorizations, the results would not look as good as those shown in Tables 5.1 and 5.2. Even though the total assignments fall short of the total authorizations, greater coordination between manpower and personnel planners in targeting a more realistic grade and skill profile could produce a relative improvement.

Right-Sizing of UTCs

At least until recently, UTCs have been sized for MTWs. Figure 5.9 shows the prevalence of UTC sizes required in the DRMDs for AEFs 1 and 2 in cycle 2. In 1,068 out of 1,733 instances, a UTC required only one position.

Table 5.3 indicates that UTCs are typically oversized for the AEFs. UTCs in the cycle 2 AEF library ranged from 1 to 517 slots, whereas the DRMDs' (demand) UTC sizes ranged from 1 to 290. The corresponding average sizes were 11.2 for the AEF library and 5.3 for the demands.

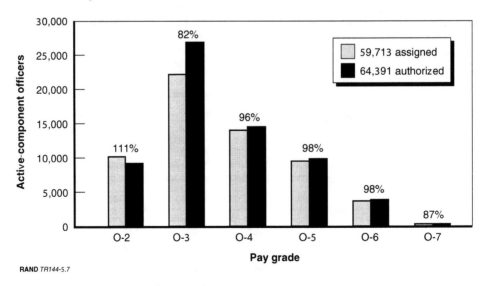

RAND TR144-5.7

Figure 5.7—Active-Component Officers in Planned Authorized Manpower and Actual Assigned Personnel

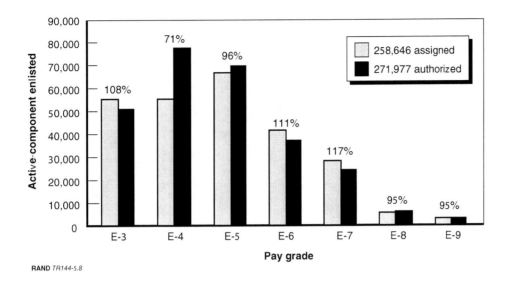

RAND *TR144-5.8*

**Figure 5.8—Active-Component Enlistees in Planned Authorized
Manpower and Actual Assigned Personnel**

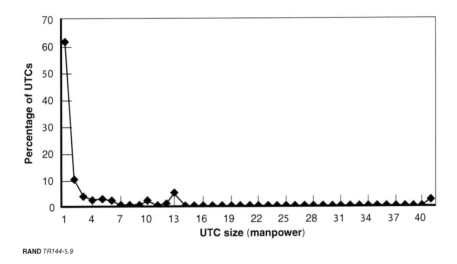

RAND *TR144-5.9*

Figure 5.9—UTC Size Profile for AEFs 1–2, Cycle 2

The response to UTC oversizing has been to use portions of UTCs as required
(tailoring). A major USAF effort continued working on making additional UTCs
available and, in particular, on delineating smaller, modular UTCs for AEF use.

Concluding Observations

At first glance, *authorizations* appeared to be adequate for the AEFs before
September 11, 2001. As noted earlier, a more in-depth look is necessary to check
whether the forces remaining at home station can meet the home station's

64

Table 5.3

UTC Size Statistics for AEFs 1 and 2, Cycle 2

| Statistic | Demand | Available Manpower | | | |
		Rotational AEF	On-Call AEW	Enablers	AEF, AEW, Enabler
Minimum	1	1	1	1	1
Maximum	290	517	517	422	517
Average	5	10	21	15	11
Standard deviation	16	34	13	37	35

remaining workload while some forces are part of an AEF rotation. In practice, the AEF Center and others must contend with various difficulties in *scheduling* manpower resources for the AEFs. Trends after September 11 still need to be analyzed to see what lasting changes have occurred that affect the EAF and related home-station requirements.

From the manpower perspective, forthcoming changes affecting UTCs are important because UTCs are the building blocks of requirements planning and estimation. Therefore, as the planned major UTC updates become official, the adequacy of the authorizations for AEFs needs to be reevaluated.

Potential Pitfalls of Using Historical SSC Demand Data

For completeness and to assist other analysts, we conclude this section with a brief review of AEF data issues that we had to attend to perform the analyses we describe in this report. To make the AEF data usable in analysis, modifications have to be made, especially to avoid double counting.

In particular, for a given rotation, the historical data are a snapshot of a database that is updated constantly as the deployment of an AEF rotation pair is first planned, then manned, then undertaken, then implemented, and finally becomes history. Arrayed after the current snapshot of information for that pair are comparable records for the next rotation pair, and so forth.

Apparently, data for the deployment of future AEF pairs are folded into the database using a previous AEF pair as a template. That means, for example, that later rotation records may be present for the Reserve and Guard in an AEF pair but might not have been finalized. (Finalization occurs as the deadline for deployment approaches.)

Furthermore, parent so-called "slick" records for a nominal 90-day period may be present along with the rotation or children records (15 days for many Reserve and Guard rotations) that together cover the 90-day period. For some of the reasons noted earlier, the children records may cover less than 90 days, and sometimes more than 90 days.

Nevertheless, after some checking, we concluded that the data are of sufficient quality to support some preliminary conclusions. We exercised care to select either parent records or children records, but not both at the same time.

6. Concluding Observations

In this section, we examine the contributions of the work we report here against the backdrop of TFA-I, for which we provided methodology improvements and extensions. We also suggest changes in the policy and in the process of a possible future TFA-like manpower-requirements-estimating exercise.

Our Extensions and Improvements to an Air Force Requirements Approach

We revised and extended TFA-I methodology to deal, albeit in a limited but important way, with scenarios that are MTW-sized but short of two MTWs. We raised the issue of what do with forces that are not tasked by the scenario chosen to drive the requirements and found a void in the requirements policy in that regard. Saying that the Air Force needs them all for all scenarios short of two MTWs would limit the possible efficiencies in the resulting requirements.

As an example of how the Air Force might fill that void, we offered a policy requiring an overseas forward presence, which treated existing overseas forces as required, regardless of whether they are included in the associated TPFDD. We suggest that the Air Force offer additional alternative policies of this type so that requirements estimation can be formalized in a logical framework.

To provide requirements methodology that could be used as the Air Force considers alternative requirements policies, we expanded the conceptual treatment of the BIM categories introduced in TFA-I to accommodate the forward-presence policy and similar policies. We took steps to make the BIM category assignment process more formal and consistent by incorporating the organizational hierarchy derived from a unit's PAS and parent PAS codes. This more-consistent classification can then be used not just with MDS authorizations but also with the TPFDD; the resulting classifications avoid many of the pitfalls in merging selected peacetime and wartime requirements to arrive at the overall requirements.

We improved an existing BIM to estimate in-place support that considers that the Reserve and Guard have part-timers. Our methodology can reduce whole untasked wings and their corresponding support. However, this approach does not account for the major force structure changes that would require changing training, wholesale logistics, or even basing. Still, it provides a first example of how the methodology can logically be expanded to fit the circumstances.

The merging methodology we provided to arrive at the overall requirements is more automated than that of TFA-I. With the help of computer programs written for that purpose, it can estimate a set of requirements in 1 to 2 hours, making it practical to perform what-if analyses and to assess alternative requirements policies. The methodology also provides a complete auditing trail both for assigning manpower to BIM categories and for the BIM adjustment method (a combination of workload, MAF, and 8-percent adjustments) selected for estimating in-place support manpower.

Overall, TFA-I and our approach, with their corresponding BIM focus on support, are methods more for estimating changes to existing requirements than for estimating manpower requirements from first principles. This is especially true because large segments of positions, such as those in the continuing mission BIM category, are passed from peacetime authorizations to wartime requirements without change. Nevertheless, the conceptual requirements framework we presented allows the use of other models for such segments,[1] just as BIM was used for support.

Although our proposed requirements methodology focuses on MTW-sized (or bigger) scenarios, we also tried to assess the adequacy of existing requirements for peacetime SSC demands. The approach we used is more consistent with a capabilities-based view of the Air Force: We checked to see whether the subset of manpower authorizations postured in the AEF library would be adequate for the peacetime SSC demands the AEFs were experiencing at the time. The approach is appropriate for a peacetime environment with no call-up of the Reserve or Guard. We used the data available for historical AEF demands at the time (late cycle 1 and early cycle 2) after checking the data for consistency.

The assumed workweek length at home base is important for estimating home-base manpower requirements. The policy on the workweek length and the corresponding wartime MAF is clearly specified for the two-MTW scenario; we suggest that the corresponding policy be specified for the AEF for a home-station workweek while some of that base's forces are deployed to an AEF. Without an explicit home-base MAF, the assumption may be that the workweek is the same as that for peacetime.

_____

[1] For example a wartime MAF could also be applied to selected groups in the continuing mission BIM category.

After September 11, changes in the planning instructions and the sustained demand for "peacetime" SSCs require reassessment of the requirements. We feel that major parts of the methodology presented here remain relevant.

Suggestions for a Future TFA-Like Requirements Exercise

Insofar as we have found opportunities for improvement to TFA-I methodology or output data, this subsection can be considered a summary of the lessons learned for the benefit of future TFA-like efforts.

Improvements in the Merge Methodology

Some potential pitfalls in TFA-I's methodology (see Appendix A) could have been and were in fact foreseen. One was the difficulty of identifying the deploying TPFDD support and merging it with the BIM output to arrive at a "TFA wartime" file without double-counting positions. Some of the difficulty arises because the TPFDD's sourcing is less than fully accurate: For example, sometimes a wing is tasked when the resource being considered is really at the squadron level. (See Appendix C, in particular, the parts about UTC sourcing and converting to manpower detail.)

However, one cause of the double-counting is an inconsistent BIM category classification, in which a FAM assigns a position in MDS to the deploying forces BIM category, while the TPFDD has the corresponding position assigned to support (a different BIM category).

To avoid this, we propose using the approach we laid out in Section 3 to assign each TPFDD demand considered to a BIM category. This approach uses the same methodological concepts to classify the TPFDD demands that it uses to classify the MDS authorizations (BIM input); this by itself would substantially reduce the possibility of double-counting. Additional improvements to the requirements estimate would result if the unit sourcing of TPFDD positions (level 4) were fully accurate. However, correcting the inaccuracies is a difficult process (see Appendix C) with the existing databases.

Continual Reexamination of Requirements Policy and the Analytic Modeling Framework Outside the TFA-Like Process

The Air Force is always evolving, and requirements methods need to represent the latest circumstances. Because the Air Force needs to provide statements of manpower requirements somewhat regularly, it needs official models for manpower requirements. At the same time, it needs an analytic framework with models for assessing the viability and effectiveness of proposed manpower policies. In performing such assessments, this analytic framework could help identify areas in which it would be beneficial to set or change requirements policy. To facilitate a smooth transition from analysis to requirements statements, the analytic models and those used for determining requirements must have mutually consistent logical frameworks.

The Air Force would be prudent, however, not to undertake investigations of proposed policies as part of an official TFA-like requirements process. Considering the stakes involved, parties may be reluctant to indulge in calculating alternative requirements. Ongoing use of the full capability to analyze alternative policies might be wise, within an existing or new Air Force research unit.

Lack of such a separate analytic framework that could predict their impact promotes reluctance to apply new policies when estimating requirements. As a result, requirements scarcely change, and the Air Force may miss the opportunity to identify more cost-effective force mixes to meet a given set of requirements. We recommend ongoing development of separate models and analyses, not just when a new requirements estimate is needed. It is unrealistic to expect development of thorough models under the time pressures of a requirements exercise, such as TFA-I.

The analytic framework needs to provide visibility into the various categories of requirements, highlighting on-call forces and those whose justification is weak—information important to decisionmakers. The methodology and implementation for estimating requirements must be flexible enough to accept other policies and ad hoc changes to support what-if investigations. Over time, as new policies are formalized, the logic of the official requirements models may be revised to coincide with that in the models used previously in separate analyses.

A Quality Control Organization

According to TFA-I's statement of goals (HQ USAF XPMR, 2000b), the results of the TFA were expected to influence the POM. It could then be inferred that the TFA results should be of high quality. Analysis of the TFA methodology can identify, from first principles, potential pitfalls. In Appendix A, the analysis of the TFA output data we received shows that the potential pitfalls translated into actual problems in the results. Therefore, we suggest that, in a TFA-like requirements exercise, an Air Force organization be made responsible for quality control of the methodology, process, and results, performing more-extensive checks and balances throughout.

Such a quality control organization would have to clarify the goals for the TFA-like exercise, providing the right balance of incentives. Because each additional requirement has a cost, economic theory can provide the basis for resource trade-offs to allocate resources more efficiently. A cost can be assigned to each additional requirement, for example, if a MAJCOM or function sets realistic upper bounds on selected resources (or perhaps a budget). We feel that resource trade-offs should start at the MAJCOM or lower levels, where a richer variety of options is available. Air Staff organizations could then concentrate on trade-offs across MAJCOMs.

Greater Feedback and Control for the Process

TFA-I gave MAJCOM FAMs the responsibility (and authority) to

- assign each manpower authorization to one of the four BIM categories
- select the BIM method (and possibly override the default inputs) to estimate in-place support, including the option to specify the in-place support level fully (referred to as the *functionally determined* method)
- provide some parameters for the selected method (e.g., workload change factor).

This assigned FAM authority had few checks and balances and an insufficient auditing trail (see Appendix A).

If the FAMs continue to set the requirements for support, it is necessary to clarify their incentives. How will the FAMs' performance be measured in a TFA-like process? Will good performance simply mean specifying greater requirements, or will it mean being able to document or make a case for the greater requirements? In TFA-I, there was no requirement for a FAM to document or make a case for greater requirements. The incentives in a TFA-like process affect the quality of the results.

TFA-I's design called for a geographically distributed process with many players local to each MAJCOM. At the time the TFA wartime requirements were reassembled, some of the data processing was done at AFMRF and some at AF/XPMR. This kind of distributed system was intended to get MAJCOM acceptance of the results, among other reasons. A distributed system, like that of TFA-I, is affected by the degree of success in training the participants to do what the TFA wants and in ensuring that the models are being used as intended. Therefore, a distributed system with many participants requires a high degree of feedback and control to make sure that it achieves its goals. With the circumstances around TFA-I, it was easy to foresee that control and accountability would be a major challenge.

For a future TFA-like process, we suggest running the BIM (or a replacement) under more-controlled conditions, requiring FAMs to document their justifications for overriding default input parameters or for setting requirements ("functionally determined") without using the default models provided.[2] To minimize theses overrides, we suggest performing a BIM classification and setting default specification of inputs more carefully, along the lines of the approach we presented in Section 3, at a selected analysis organization, where quality control can be more strict. Even before the FAMs receive the default BIM classification and model parameter input data, the analysis organization can compute a preliminary set of overall results, which would expedite fixing any problems in the methodology at an early stage of the process.

Furthermore, we suggest that more automated feedback be provided as the TFA-like process progresses, giving summary reports at all levels (for FAMs, for MAJCOMs, and for Air Staff) to illuminate any possible inconsistencies in assumptions or data and, thus, to trigger corrective action.

More Model Automation and Clarification of the Logic

BIM is only one part of the requirements-estimation process. Automation of TFA-I's BIM calculations was an improvement over previous Air Force requirements-estimation efforts because it speeded up the process. However, other TFA-I steps, such as "the merge" of BIM output with deployed support, would also have benefited from additional automation.

The last step in TFA-I's requirements estimation was to merge the BIM output with TPFDD support demands. The logic of this step either was incomplete or lacked sufficient information to operate on, leading to an error-prone, manually intensive process, with little automation (see Appendix A). The time-consuming merge was carried out at least twice, because problems became apparent after the first round. In the end, time pressures (the results were already being used for the TFCFR) led to the acceptance of the results in spite of remaining problems.

---

[2] At a more basic level, immediate checks for reasonable model inputs should be provided, such as requiring explanations for values that are outside of predetermined acceptable ranges.

It is our experience that attempting to automate a process, such as by writing a computer program performing the various steps, helps by making explicit and thus documenting the full logic required for the process. Furthermore, comprehensive testing of the automation tool will help reveal bad or incomplete logic that needs revision. It is in this context, as well to speed up the process, that we feel that automation of the merging is necessary.

A Perspective on Model Limitations in General

We end this section with a philosophical acknowledgment of the limitations of models in general. For complicated systems, models cannot be all-encompassing tools for arriving at an answer. Decisionmakers must know the strengths and limitations of the models, their data, and the assumptions and decide whether to accept the model results. Even when the results are accepted, adjustments may be needed to reflect aspects of the real world that the models do not consider (e.g., political issues or transition during implementation).

Appendix

A. Opportunities for Other Improvements in the Total Force Assessment

As motivation for the proposed improvements we presented in Section 3, Section 2 commented on the potential pitfalls of TFA-I. The comments in Section 2 came from an analysis of the TFA-I's methodology and process. In Section 4, we compared some of the results that used either our proposed methodology or that of TFA-I. This appendix goes further, and in more detail, to show not only the potential problems but actual troublesome results in TFA-I. We based these on our study and analysis of the TFA documents (HQ USAF XPMR, 2000b; HQ USAF XPMR, 2000a), TFA-I's BIM software (AFMIA, 2000), and its input (AFMRF, 2001a; AFMIA, 2001a) and output files (AFMRF.2001d; AFMIA.2001b). Recommendations for addressing these problems appear in Section 6.

The Merge Leading to the TFA-I "Wartime File" Requirements

We will begin by reviewing the BIM category codes actually used in the output files, which will allow us to be more precise. Next, we will review the TFA-I input and output data for the Reserve and Guard, then those for the active component.

BIM Categories for TFA-I

TFA-I's BIM output file used the following four categories of manpower:

- deploying forces (coded as *DEF*)
- in-place combat forces (coded as *INF*)
- continuing mission (coded as *INM*)
- in-place support (coded as *INS*).

Note that, although HQ USAF XPMR (2000b) had specified using *DEP* as the identifier for deploying forces, the actual TFA-I BIM output file and the TFA-I actual requirements file (the TFA wartime file) instead used *DEF*. The TFA wartime file does use DEP but in reference to the TFA TPFDD's (deploying) support demands; in this appendix we follow the latter usage.

In the next two sections, we use Figure A.1 and Table A.1 to describe the progression (from left to right) of the various manpower positions, from MDS authorizations leading to the TFA wartime requirements (in fact, they combine some peacetime and wartime requirements).

Figure A.1 shows that, in theory, TFA-I support requirements result from merging the BIM output with the TFA TPFDD support. Even though Figure A.1 does not show the authorizations in the categories of deploying forces, in-place combat forces, or continuing missions as inputs to TFA-I's BIM, they did go through the TFA-I BIM and, in theory, came out unchanged (straightlined).[1]

Table A.1 shows, for broad component categories, the MDS authorizations (BIM input), the BIM output, and the changes (plus or minus) between input and output. The last column shows the final requirements from the TFA wartime file (AFMRF, 2001c). The next-to-last column is the result of subtracting the DEP increment added in the merge step from the final totals. The difference between the TFA wartime results (AFMRF, 2001c) and the BIM output is, in theory, only the part of the TFA TPFDD identified as deploying support.

TFA Data for Reserve and Guard and Potential Problems

In Table A.1, starting with the Guard MDS authorizations (113,373) and leading to the BIM output (65,001), we note a drastic reduction of close to half the starting value. Furthermore, the full TFA wartime requirement is even smaller (56,281) than the BIM output. There is an inconsistency in the process here because the TFA wartime file is supposed to include the BIM output and the DEP deploying support increment. We brought this unexplained drastic change to the Air Force's attention in October 2001 but could not get an explanation other than an acknowledgment that there were some problems with the TFA wartime file. The precipitous drop between the BIM output and the TFA wartime file without the DEP increment is circumstantial evidence of problems, e.g., either an error or a reclassification of BIM categories in the TFA wartime file.

A similar review for the Reserve starts with 61,640 MDS authorizations, drops by about one-third to 40,512 in the BIM output, and bounces back to within a minute fraction of its starting value (within 0.21 of 1 percent). For the Reserve,

---

[1] As we note below for the Guard, there is a possibility that some errors occurred that caused a change in these categories.

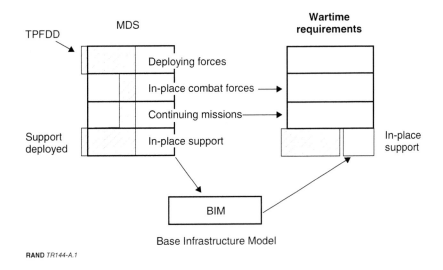

Base Infrastructure Model

RAND *TR144-A.1*

Figure A.1—Overview of TFA-I's Requirements Methodology

Table A.1

Tracking MDS Positions Through BIM Input to TFA-I Requirements

Identifying Attributes				Changes			TFA-I Wartime Requirements	
Mil/ Civ	Type	Component	MDS[a] Auths.	Plus	Minus	BIM Out	w/o DEP[b]	w/DEP[c]
Mil		Active	327,783	3,395	35,226	294,620	299,907	342,609
Mil		Reserve	61,640	106	21,234	40,512	40,512	61,515
Mil		Guard	113,373	391	48,739	65,001	27,800	56,281
Mil		IMA	2,201	0	2,201	0	1,470[d]	1,470[d]
Civ	CME		81,086	2	19	81,069	81,587	81,587
Civ	DMC		1,073	1	37	1,037	1,037	1,037
Civ			129,796	196	3,180	128,168	127,022	127,032
Total			716,952	4,091	110,636	610,407	577,865	671,531

SOURCE: TFA-I's BIM input and MDS (AFMRF, 2001a), BIM output (AFMRF, 2001d), and resulting requirements (AFMRF, 2001c).

[a]MDS record counts exclude classified records.

[b]TFA-I's requirements without the DEP increment include only the positions that are classified as DEF, INF, INM, or INS.

[c]TFA-I's requirements with DEP include all BIM categories, including the DEP deploying support increment. A total of 8,727 unsourced positions (from the 9,329 unsourced TPFDD demands) are coded as DEP in the TFA wartime file. We included the 8,725 military positions as part of the active component (the other two are civilian).

[d]At least 1,470 IMA could be traced in the TFA-I's requirements.

the BIM output and the TFA wartime requirements without the DEP increment are identical, in great contrast to the Guard.

Some positions that were in one category in the BIM output were switched to another category in the TFA-I's requirements. This happened at AF/XPMR in some cases, at times with Air Staff FAM input. Thus, the category information the MAJCOM FAMs provided was at times overridden. In the best of cases, the reclassification had no major effect other than providing a different perception of a function for reporting purposes. A skeptical reviewer, however, can see the potential for unintended use, in which one category can be chosen to obtain a certain BIM effect. For example, the idea may be to classify authorizations where they were least likely to be cut, and, when the resulting characterization draws attention, to change the category but leave the requirements as is. We suggest that reclassifying BIM categories after generating the BIM output require an explanation and an audit trail.

The BIM outputs for the Reserve and Guard do show a drop of between one-third and one-half from the starting MDS positions, telling us that the BIM model and the process that uses it warrant close attention. The requirements process might not have represented either the model or the process applied to the ARC adequately. The facts that the TFA wartime requirement for the Reserve returned to the MDS value, where it started, and the factual reclassification of BIM categories could together be indications that attempts were made to compensate for deficiencies in the methodology dealing with the ARC.

In Section 3, we attempted to improve how BIM handles the Reserve and Guard. Analysis of the methodology made the need for these improvements clear, and the above quantitative review of the TFA data simply reinforced that need.

TFA Data for the Active Component and Problems in TFA-I's Methodology for Merging

For the active component, the BIM output and TFA-I's wartime requirements with the DEP support increment differ by almost 50,000 positions. This increment, in theory, should include only the deploying support in the TPFDD to be added to the BIM output (see Figure A.1). As noted in footnote c to Table A.1, 8,725 (17 percent) of these 50,000 are unsourced. The DEP classification of the unsourced demands is consistent with the finding (see Table A.2) that they are mainly in support. However, the unsourced DEP positions include 163 pilot specialties (AFSCs beginning with 011) in nonaviation UTCs, as well as approximately 600 positions in maintenance UTCs.

In any case, if untasked MDS authorizations could be tasked to meet unsourced demands, adding these to requirements exaggerates the result. Unsourced TPFDD demands may mean only that the TPFDD sourcing was not complete.

Table A.2

Breakout of Unsourced UTCs in the TFA TPFDD

UTC First Character		Manpower	%	Cum %	Pilots AFS = 011
F	Medical dental	1,975	21	21	
6	Communications, communications maintenance, electronics signal	1,430	15	36	
U	Transportation/cargo handling, motor	1,078	12	48	
4	Engineer, TOPO service	1,040	11	59	
J	Supply, supply support services	945	10	69	
H	Maintenance, ship development— construction and maintenance	779	8	78	
C	Command headquarters, DOD agencies	692	7	85	79
X	Posts, camps, rescue, weather, stations, base	378	4	89	72
7	Tactical control, weather, rescue, command and control	357	4	93	39
P	Intelligence, counter intelligence	308	3	96	
9	Miscellaneous combat, combat support, and combat service support	286	3	99	29
Q	Military police, security, law enforcement	59	1	100	
R	Personnel, admin, information, Reserve forces	2	0	100	
	TOTAL	9,329	100		219

SOURCE: AFMRF (2001b) .

Identification of sourced TPFDD support (DEP is deployed support) is not straightforward. It requires paying attention to how the MAJCOM FAMs have assigned MDS positions to BIM categories. In particular, it is important not to incorrectly identify a TPFDD position as support to be added to the BIM output as DEP when, it fact, that position is already in the BIM output classified as deploying forces. Failure to catch such misidentifications result in double counting.[2]

---

[2] Our proposed methodology suggests some improvements for the merging methodology to make it arrive at the combined requirements (the equivalent of the TFA wartime file). The proposed methodology requires performing a BIM classification of not only the MDS but also the TPFDD (see Section 3) and using that information while merging the data to avoid double-counting requirements.

Even when TPFDD positions had been sourced, and, therefore, the UIC was known, it could be difficult to determine whether a TPFDD position was already included in the BIM output because problems with inaccurate sourcing are not uncommon (see Section 3 and Appendix C). For example, sometimes a headquarters unit (which would normally be classified as support) may be tasked to provide certain resources for a TPFDD when the resources actually belong to a related squadron of deploying forces, which would have already passed straight to the BIM output. If such inaccurate sourcing is not caught during the merging process, the positions could be added into the total a second time. AFMRF staff who merged the data knew of this potential problem and, we were told, tried to avoid creating additional requirements.

Furthermore, even when the sourcing was done to the right unit, it is difficult to determine whether or not all positions of that unit were already in the BIM output. This would require checking overall totals or checking one position at the time—a tedious, time-consuming process, especially because the process was not automated (the logic was incomplete, and there are many special cases). Ensuring that the BIM output accounts for all deploying TPFDD positions for a unit deciding on an appropriate DEP increment is even more complicated when support units (or just portions of the functional groups, FACs, or AFSCs) have been straightlined. Because the TFA-I merging took place at a more aggregate level than the BIM output's position level of detail, it was difficult to ascertain what was straightlined and what was not.

It is difficult to measure the prevalence of double-counted positions within the DEP increment to the BIM output. Our examination of the "tattler" file (more on that below) revealed only many symptoms of problems. One way to get an aggregate measure is to look at certain specialty groups and compare the TFA wartime totals with the starting MDS. We have done that for some specialties or career fields[3] in the figures below.

Figure A.2 illustrates the requirements for active-component fighter pilots. TFA-I's requirements for this important specialty group exceeded the MDS authorizations, again mainly in the support category. For the sake of comparison, requirements we estimated using our proposed methodology for the 2-MTW+DEF scenario are also shown (as well as those for some one-MTW scenarios).

---

[3] We used a mapping from the Air Force's 2001 Total Force Career Field Review (TFCFR) to identify career fields based on the significant first three characters of AFSCs.

The requirements for TFA-I's scenario exceeded the MDS authorizations noticeably for pilots and maintenance (see Figures A.2 and A.3) and substantially for transportation (see Figure A.4). In October 2001, we informed Air Force

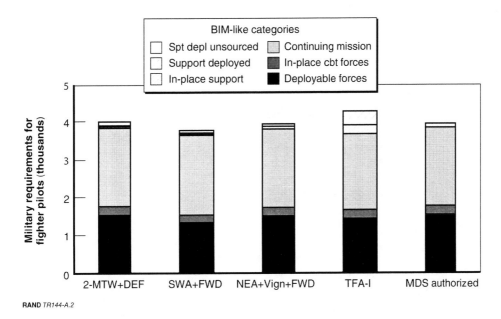

**Figure A.2—Active-Component Military Requirements for
Fighter Pilots for Alternative Scenarios**

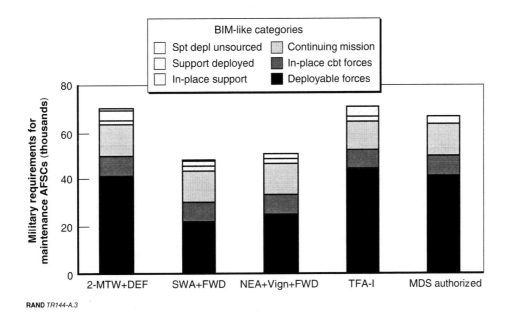

**Figure A.3—Active-Component Military Requirements for
Maintenance for Alternative Scenarios**

82

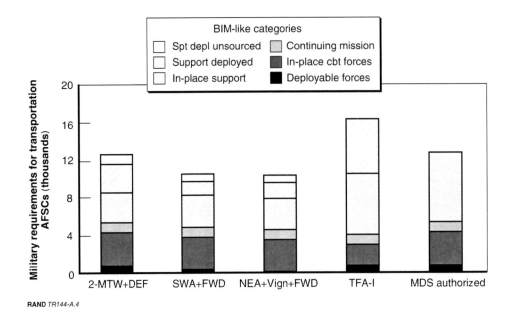

RAND TR144-A.4

**Figure A.4—Active-Component Military Requirements for
Transportation for Alternative Scenarios**

representatives of the pilots' results, and they agreed that some adjustments were necessary.

In summary, there may be good reasons that TFA-I had some unintuitive results. However, the evidence mounts that the TFA-I results had certain specific problems.

Our analyses revealed the following:

- The methodology and process had significant potential pitfalls because the TFA process was distributed and had weak controls (see Section 2 and the review of tattler data later in this appendix).

- The methodology for identifying deploying support, with or without unsourced TPFDD records, also presented significant potential pitfalls.

- In the actual TFA-I data, there were drastic changes between the MDS authorizations and the BIM output and on to the TFA wartime file, especially for the Reserve and Guard.

- In the actual TFA-I wartime requirements the requirements in selected specialties (pilots and maintenance, for example) had noticeable unexplained increments in the support category in comparison with the MDS authorizations. These are consistent with the difficulty of identifying TPFDD deploying support DEP that is not already in the BIM output. The Air Force acknowledged that the pilot requirements needed adjustments.

These potential and actual problems translate into a requirements statement that needs further strengthening.

The rest of this appendix presents other comments about the TFA-I data, its methodology, and process with a view to providing a list of minor lessons learned that may be useful in a future TFA-like process.

Other Minor Discrepancies in the TFA Files

As Table A.1 indicates, the BIM input or MDS authorizations did include CMEs, Deutsche-mark and United Kingdom civilians (DMCs), and some IMAs. The CMEs and DMCs should have passed through the system unchanged, but in fact either new positions were added ("Plus" column) or some authorizations were deleted ("Minus" column) before arriving at the BIM output ("BIM Out" column).

The approximate increase of 500 CMEs between the BIM output and the TFA wartime file (TFA-I "w/o DEP" column) stands out. The increase is caused by 544 civilian positions that were reclassified as CMEs, even though making such changes was not part of the overarching guidance for the TFA or within its scope (HQ USAF XPMR, 2000b).

The original TFA guidance on IMA positions was to leave them out of the BIM input file, and this is what was done for most of the MAJCOMs. One of the primary purposes of IMA positions is to provide for wartime fill-ins for essential at-home positions that deploying warfighters are vacating. Since the purpose of the TFA process was to calculate the wartime requirements, one of the outcomes would have been to identify the wartime in-place positions that IMAs might fill. This would have been done after the BIM processing and TPFDD merge were completed.

But when the Air Force Materiel Command (AFMC) analysts ran the BIM, they noted that large numbers of AFMC's "wartime IMA" requirements had been deleted by the exclusion of IMAs from the BIM input file. The command believed it should be allowed to keep the wartime IMAs as part of its wartime in-place requirement. We are uncertain about what the rules were for dealing with IMAs after this issue was raised, but about 2,200 IMA positions remained in the BIM input file (out of about 10,000 in the original MDS database). Although none of the IMA positions made their way into the BIM output file, at least 1,470 IMA positions (almost all of them from AFMC) were included in the final TFA output (wartime) file. This brings attention to other possible use of IMAs in the Air Force: As a way of obtaining military experts part-time who may not be available full-time. Future TFA-like efforts may have to include these IMAs in the requirements-estimation process, classified as continuing mission requirements.

Incomplete Audit Trail of How BIM Was Used

The TFA's tattler file (AFMIA, 2001b) was intended to provide an audit trail for the BIM input choices that the MAJCOM FAMs made for running TFA-I's BIM. We next discuss the serious limitations of using the tattler file as an audit trail.

Problems in Using the BIM Tattler File in Analysis

The tattler file did not track all the records of the BIM input or output. Reportedly, the tattler file contained a record only if the BIM input for some part of the organization's manpower was labeled as in-place support. So, in theory, there was no tattler record when the entire unit was labeled as DEF, INF, or INM.

When a set of changes summarizable in one tattler file record was applied to a group of manpower authorizations covering multiple FACs, organization kinds, or types, an asterisk was written in some field(s) of the tattler file record. That made it difficult or impossible to link these changes to the BIM input file for tracking. For example, if a certain factor were applied to several FACs within a unit, there might be only one unit-level tattler record; an asterisk in the FAC field of that record would denote some subsidiary FACs had been changed, but not which ones.

Furthermore, multiple records could be written for a given group of manpower positions, thus requiring the data analyst to be careful to include only the record with the most recent time stamp. Apparent reruns of BIM for some MAJCOMs may explain the presence of some multiple records.

Selection of BIM Support Adjustment Method

TFA-I used various BIM support adjustment methods, most commonly the following:[4]

- reducing manpower by applying wartime MAF factors
- keeping manpower constant (that is, straightlining)

---

[4] BIM support adjustment methods other than those listed here (base population supported, gallons dispensed, and primary aircraft inventory) generated too few records to be discernable in most charts in this appendix.

- applying the 8 percent of TPFDD deployer factor (to account for changes in base mission population) or some related percentage, through the BIM Factor Calculator (BFC)

- applying FAM-directed ("functionally determined") changes that override any other potential adjustments.

The MAJCOM FAMs selected one of these methods when they provided the BIM inputs for a group of manpower positions.

The "functionally determined" method bypasses the standard adjustments in the workweek or adjustments for changes in mission population. In this method, the MAJCOM FAM sets the in-place support manpower to the desired quantity. Presumably, the FAMs entered their best estimates, higher or lower than the current MDS value.

The BFC was an algorithm that the FAM could run separately from the BIM and that allowed them to enter the results into the BIM output manually. The TFA-I BFC could be used to apportion the 8-percent reduction for deployers to the various BOS organizations. One approach used a pro rata factor, and another used FAM-provided factors. However, the user could override the BFC factor results and instead enter his or her best estimate, and that was apparently done in some cases.

BIM users who overrode the default assumptions (e.g., by choosing the functionally determined method) were not required to justify their actions (such as by providing notes in the tattler file). We suggest more stringent controls in this regard in future TFA-like processes.

Lacking a separate file explaining why a method was selected or why a given factor input is appropriate, the TFA tattler file, even after removing the obvious duplicate records, can only provide anecdotal evidence of the problems we have inferred or found through other means.

B. Comparison of BIM Classification Systems

This appendix compares the results of the RAND and TFA-I approaches for MDS BIM classification. We also provide more details on the RAND approach. This and additional classification results, which are based on MAJCOM or even PAS code, are available in a computer file for the Air Force's review and comment.

Figure B.1 shows that, in aggregate terms, RAND's proposed classification system comes close to that of TFA-I's when applied to active-component positions in the MDS. Because it cannot be discerned from the TFA-I BIM data, certain MDS authorizations not present in the BIM output file are presumed to be support (labeled as "Deleted: BOS?" in Figure B.1). It is highly likely that these positions were deleted while the BIM was adjusting for wartime's longer workweek. It is less likely that authorizations were deleted if the related workload was set to zero. (However, some deletions may have been accidental.)

However, for the Guard and Reserve, the difference between the results of the classification systems is noticeable for some BIM categories, as Figures B.2 and B.3 show. For the Guard, the totals of the first three BIM categories (deployable forces, in-place forces, continuing mission) are rather close; the major differences are mainly in the split between deployable and in-place combat forces.

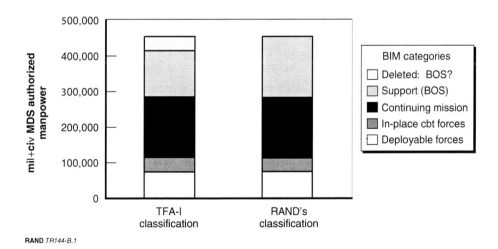

RAND TR144-B.1

Figure B.1—Comparison of BIM Classification Systems for MDS Active-Component Authorizations

88

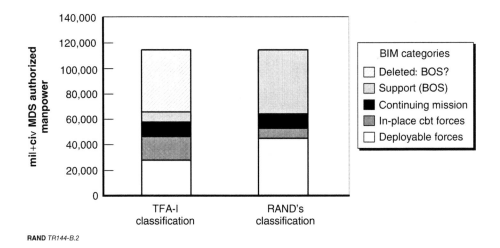

Figure B.2—Comparison of BIM Classification Systems for
MDS Guard Authorizations

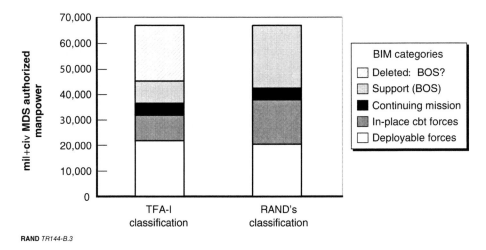

Figure B.3—Comparison of BIM Classification
Systems for MDS Reserve Authorizations

For the Reserve, the two classification systems appear to differ by virtue of a net shift of BOS or deleted authorizations for in-place combat forces. For the two-MTW scenario, the two BIM methodologies concentrate on adjusting the support category (because the combat forces are assumed to be required, as are those with a continuing mission; see Sections 2 and 3). Therefore, for that scenario, there are the major differences in Reserve manpower requirements (see Figure 4.7) in the estimated support category.

In an effort to provide more details on our BIM classification method, we provide Table B.1, which lists the ORG kinds and types that determine a unit's BIM classification (see also Table 3.2).

Table B.1

Assignment of Manpower Positions in Organizational Units to BIM-Like Categories

BIM Category	ORG Kind and ORG Type
Deployable forces (16 entries)	abcsq, acwft, alcsq, aosft, cegft, cstgp, eigsq, elksq, hgnsq, itlft, mlmgp, mmasq, opcft, stpft, stpgp, stpsq
In-place forces (22 entries)	adfsq, alsgp, alssq, avsft, ccosq, helft, helsq, itssq, iwsft, mafsq, mccsq, moesq, mslsq, munsq, nedsq, sedsq, sfsof, slssq, ssvsq, swnsq, wadsq, wersq
Continuing mission (617 entries)	*ac, *ag, *ap, *bd, *bl, *ce, *cl, *cm, *cr, *do, *dt, *du, *fe, *fo, *gd, *hq, *hs, *in, *jo, *jq, *js, *lb, *me, *mu, *sa, *sc, *sr, *st, *un, *ut, acuft, acusq, acwsq, adbof, adssq, afssq, airft, airgp, airsq, aitft, aitgp, asaof, aspdv, atesq, bdaof, cboft, cbosq, cbpft, cbpsq, ccvgp, cresq, crpgp, cttsq, edugp, edusq, ewfgp, ewfsq, exrsq, exsdv, fmtsq, ftagp, ftasq, ftssq, fwpsq, hmswg, iopsq, iopwg, itlwg, matsq, mdogp, mdpgp, mdtgp, megwg, mlcof, mpift, mpkft, mscgp, msggp, prrft, q*, rdxsq, recgp, recsq, repft, revsq, rmoof, rncsq, rsdsq, rsqft, rssft, rsssq, rtdrg, rterg, rtfrg, rtnrg, samdv, scrof, sefgp, segof, smudv, spogp, sscgp, ssssq, stuft, stusq, swxsq, syosq, tepsq, tesgp, teswg, tevgp, tevsq, tkaof, trgft, trggp, tsssq, tsysq, weggp, x*, z*
Support (48 entries)	absgp, abssq, abswg, acnwg, adtsq, alfgp, arfgp, arfwg, bmbwg, ceggp, consq, cprft, cprsq, crggp, eiggp, fdirg, fdisq, ftrgp, gctft, grpgp, lgsdv, loggp, lopgp, lstdv, lstft, lstsq, mbywg, mdssq, medgp, megft, meggp, megsq, msqft, pspsq, rcnwg, rsqgp, rsqwg, scsft, sefft, seoft, serft, sfpft, sopgp, sopwg, supft, supsq, trsft, trssq

NOTE: An asterisk acts as a "wild card" character, in this case to stand in place of one or more characters.

C. TPFDD Data Pitfalls That Affect Requirements Estimation

A TPFDD file serves many purposes, from planning the timing of deployments to documenting the day-by-day personnel and cargo lift requirements for deployments. The Air Force also uses the TPFDD, in concert with the MANFOR file, to specify TPFDD manpower requirements with details down to specific manpower categories (AFSC, FAC, etc.).

Various problems in the construction, identification, and documentation of UTCs and TPFDDs complicate requirements determination or in some degree limit the validity of the results. This appendix draws attention to those problems for the benefit of other analysts and in the hope that the Air Force will make improvements for future TPFDDs, especially if they are to be used for estimating overall manpower requirements:

- **TPFDDs documentation may be sparse and difficult to find.** Typically TPFDD files have little separate documentation about how scenario goals were implemented in the TPFDD construction. For the TFA, the two-MTW TPFDD documentation included the overarching guidance (HQ USAF XPMR, 2000b) and an AF/XOPW briefing (Fisher, 2000). That documentation was insufficient for understanding the TFA-peculiar codes used during its construction. Luckily, in this instance, we were able to contact a key person who participated in building the TPFDD, who provided us with additional details (the meanings of patterns in ULN codes). In general, a deeper understanding of the conventions used in the construction of a TPFDD has to be extracted through reverse-engineering the TPFDD file itself.

- **TPFDDs may include in-place or on-call forces.** One difficulty with identifying in-place or on-call forces is that the conventions that, in theory, identify them may vary even within a single TPFDD or may not be followed all the time. This lack of consistency means that there is a risk of misidentifying TPFDD units that are on call or in other categories.

  TPFDDs typically include not only units planned for deployment but also some that are either in-place or on-call units. The code Z in the mode-code field may identify an in-place unit. But sometimes in-place units can only be identified as those having identical origin and destination geographic location codes (GEOLOCs) or when the origin GEOLOC is missing.

Various conventions are also used to identify on-call units. Sometimes their RDDs are either set to *999* or left blank; other times, the descriptions of their GEOLOC codes refer to unknown destinations (sometimes the country is specified, but not the base or location). The latter appears to be the case in the TFA TPFDD, where the RDD field was missing.

- **Nonstandard UTCs may lack manpower position details.** TPFDDs may include UTC packages whose identifying five-character code ends with *Z99*, indicating that they are not standard or have not yet been approved. Unless the TPFDD already has AFSC-level detail for the *Z99* UTCs, their manpower at the AFSC level cannot be readily determined. If a Z99 UTC does not have AFSC-level detail, the stated requirement is essentially meaningless as an input to the determination of wartime manpower requirements.

- **UTC sourcing may be incomplete or inaccurate.** Sometimes the UTC sourcing is missing (left blank): No organizational unit (identified by its UIC) is tasked to provide the manpower resources.[1] Even if a UIC is identified, the unit may not have all the resources specified in the MANFOR, which means the sourcing is inaccurate. Sometimes, however, the resources can be found in a parent or wing-level organization at the same base, or the wing-level organization may be tasked while the resources are available only in its subordinate units. At worst, the desired capability may be filled by a person from somewhere else on the unit's base, possibly part of a different MAJCOM.

  One way to correct these sourcing inaccuracies is to fragment the UTC, assigning parts of it to the actual units that have the required UTC resources. Some of the fragmenting we observed (TPFDDs and AEF library) occurred when resources were required from two MAJCOMs, e.g., in aviation UTCs for AWACS and JSTARS. Clearly, when estimating the aviation aircraft and manpower resources used by a given TPFDD, fragmented aviation UTCs need to be handled carefully to prevent double-counting.

  These sourcing problems make it very difficult to ascertain whether there are overtaskings or shortages relative to the MDS authorizations. Requiring proper sourcing of all UTCs in a TPFDD would force its creators to check resource availability. A corollary is that failing to source UTCs opens the possibility that insufficient resources will be available to source these UTCs.

- **Intra-CONUS deployments may lead to double-counting or to an increase of base mission population.** A TPFDD may include movements of units

---

[1] For example, this occurs in UTCs for approximately 9,300 out of some 215,000 total positions in the two-MTW TPFDD for TFA-I.

whose origin and destination are both in CONUS. Unsuspecting TPFDD users may end up double-counting manpower if the same TPFDD includes an intra-CONUS deployment *followed by* a subsequent deployment outside the CONUS.

In theory, intra-CONUS deployments could lead to a net increase in the mission population BOS must support. If so, base-support estimating methods need to handle these "negative" deployments.

Intra-CONUS deployments that are not followed by deployment outside the CONUS raise the issue of whether these demands should be filled by military personnel (current UTCs overwhelmingly required military personnel). For these deployments, a review is in order to look for opportunities that use civilian instead of military personnel.

- **Inclusion of mobility deployments may double-count some TPFDD demands.** A TPFDD may call for successive short-term deployments of the same mobility forces. Steps need to be taken to avoid the double-counting of the related resources.

- **Pitfalls in converting UTC-level TPFDDs to manpower details.** Unless a TPFDD is actually executed, TPFDDs are normally constructed, sourced, and fragmented at the UTC level (level 2), not at the manpower position level (level 4). Converting a UTC-level TPFDD to include manpower position details requires using the MANFOR file with UTC manpower definitions. Care must be exercised not to assign the full set of UTC resources to each individual portion of a single fragmented UTC, which would lead to double-counting of manpower resources. The resulting level-4 UTCs may require sourcing adjustments because the UICs they inherit from the UTC-level sourcing are, in general, representative but sometimes inaccurate. As noted earlier, the UIC may point to a wing and not to the actual unit that has the manpower resources.

The effort required to fix inaccurate sourcings at the manpower position level is not trivial and, therefore, not typically made. In principle, the sourcing of the TPFDD can be redone and would involve "aligning" TPFDD positions to MDS positions. If a TPFDD position cannot be found in the specified UIC, there should be a search (with the help of a computer program) for available matching AFSCs (and FACs) in other organizations of the same wing or, if not there, elsewhere on the same base and in the MAJCOM, and so on, extending (by relaxing the FAC, for example) the search domain each time. The methodology is understandably somewhat complicated, but approximations can be made. In the past, RAND has done this kind of alignment but only at a more aggregate 3-character AFSC level to allow for some AFSC substitutions.

- **Extracting aircraft force strength from the TPFDD is difficult.** One important measure of the size of demands that a particular TPFDD reflects is the implied aircraft requirement. Using the TPFDD's UTC description fields to get a total of the various aircraft types supported is problematic. The process requires parsing the UTC description fields to get the correct aircraft information, which is tedious at best. If the TPFDD file already has AFSC (level 4) details, reverse engineering is required to get the UTC package counts (a level-2 detail file) for use in deriving the aircraft count.

  Then, the fragmentation problem just noted for manpower presents the possibility of double-counting, because the full UTC *aircraft* quantity is also sometimes reported for each related instance of a fragmented UTC. In addition, some UTCs may report only the aircraft and some only the pilots and crews associated with that unit type. It is then necessary to exclude the pilot- and crew-only UTCs, which can be identified only by parsing the description field.

- **TPFDD UTCs may not be right-sized.** A TPFDD can sometimes be inconsistent in that a UTC description field sometimes indicates that it supports a certain number of aircraft and at other times a different number. This may occur because old TPFDDs are often the starting points for new ones. A UTC originally designed to support a certain number of aircraft may be used later to support fewer, e.g., the squadron size is reduced. In actual use, UTC tailoring solves the problem by tasking only the personnel required: this is done frequently in the AEF environment. However, using full UTCs in planning for smaller squadrons potentially exaggerates the requirement.

- **TPFDDs may be inconsistent with existing mobility resources.** Some TPFDDs may not have been checked to see whether enough mobility assets are available to make transporting them feasible, making these TPFDDs less realistic. Checking for transportation feasibility was beyond the scope of our work.

D. MDS Authorizations Whose Requirements Need to Be Estimated Elsewhere

A few categories of manpower either are estimated using separate methods or are not appropriate for inclusion in our modeling; this appendix discusses them. These categories need to be estimated and tracked separately; whether they should be included in overall manpower requirements depends on the context. With the exceptions of DMCs (see below), we have excluded these categories from our models but refer to them occasionally in our analysis of Air Force data.

- **Contractor Manpower-Equivalents.** The MDS database includes CMEs as a means of accounting for Air Force workloads that are performed on contract instead of by organic (military and/or civilian) personnel. It is widely acknowledged that the CME numbers in the MDS do not correspond directly to the numbers of contractor personnel working on Air Force installations (or even with the numbers of personnel actually employed to cover contracted workloads). That is especially true for workloads that have been on contract for more than a few years.[1] MDS CME numbers are crude measures, at best, of the number and types of personnel that would be required if the Air Force were to perform the contracted workloads organically. We believe that, in calculating wartime requirements, these resources should be accounted for, but the CME data are of such questionable validity that they cannot be used as a basis for such calculations. We have excluded CMEs from our models, but report their MDS totals when needed.

- **Individual Mobilization Augmentees.** In principle, one type of IMA fills positions that would be left vacant by deployers in wartime; their numbers could be reestimated after the total requirements become available. Another type of IMA is used as a way to obtain military experts part-time who may not be available as full-time personnel. In the requirements-estimation process, these IMAs could be assigned to the continuing mission BIM category.

---

[1] CME data are typically entered in the MDS when a contract is let but not corrected when other authorizations are updated later.

Following the choice of TFA-I, we excluded IMAs from consideration in our approach, except in a few instances for the sake of comparison.[2]

- **Reserve and Guard Civilian Technicians.** Normally, these technicians are represented in the MDS by two records: one for their full-time civilian status and one for their corresponding military drill (part-time) authorizations. Because TFA-I's two-MTW scenario and our scenarios with at least one MTW assume full mobilization of the Reserve and Guard, these authorizations would become full-time military during an MTW. Therefore, we and the Air Force have done our best to remove such civilian technician records from the BIM input file; this process is imperfect at best, because many of the Guard civilian authorizations in the MDS cannot be matched against their drill counterparts.

- **Deutsche-Mark and United Kingdom Civilians.** Foreign host countries pay for about 1,000 DMCs (Germany or the United Kingdom). We included them without change in the requirements shown in earlier sections.

- **Students and Trainees.** Air Force total manpower requirements include student, trainee, and cadet positions, some of which are listed in part in the MDS file's part d. Normally these (peacetime) requirements would be estimated either as fixed requirements (e.g., academy cadets) or as a percentage of total other military requirements (e.g., transients). They fall outside the main focus of this document. Therefore, in dealing with MDS data, we omitted part d of the file.

---

[2] In Appendix A, we noted that, in TFA-I, some AFMC IMAs were added back to the TFA wartime file.

References

Aerospace Expeditionary Force (AEF) Center, AEF/AES, "2nd Cycle Sourcing Approval Conference Outbrief," briefing, Langley AFB, Va., October 2000a.

_____, AEF historical data, file RAND.mdb, Langley AFB, Va., December 1, 2000b.

AFMIA, Base Infrastructure Model (BIM), file Bim0712.exe, Randolph AFB, Tex., July 12, 2000.

_____, BIM deployer data, file BFC.xls, Randolph AFB, Tex., January 8, 2001a.

_____, BIM tattler data, file Tattler_Files.exe, Randolph AFB, Tex., April 23, 2001b.

Air Force Manpower Readiness Flight (AFMRF), miscellaneous data, including AEF library cycle 2, Site R, Ft. Detrick, Md., July 20, 2000a.

_____, AEF historical data, file Randssc.mdb, Site R, Ft. Detrick, Md., September 7, 2000b.

_____, Base Infrastructure Model (BIM) input data, files bim part1.mdb to bim part7.mdb, Site R, Ft. Detrick, Md., January 19, 2001a.

_____, Total Force Assessment (TFA) Time-Phased Force and Deployment Data (TPFDD), file contractor_tfa_tpfdd.mdb, Site R, Ft. Detrick, Md., April 20, 2001b.

_____, TFA Wartime data, version 3, file wartime_3.mdb, Site R, Ft Detrick, Md., April 20, 2001c.

_____, BIM output data, version 2, file BIM_2.zip, Site R, Ft. Detrick, Md., April 25, 2001d.

_____, AFWUS data, file AFWUS(RAND).mdb, Site R, Ft. Detrick, Md., January 8, 2002.

Fisher, Lt Col Steve, "TFA Deployment Process," AF/XOPW, briefing given at TFA Workshop, San Antonio, Tex., June 7, 2000.

Headquarters, Air Force Personnel Center DPSA, assigned personnel data, Randolph AFB, Tex., 2000. Online at http://www.afpc.randolph.af.mil/sasdemog/Ideas_pre_sel.

Headquarters U.S. Air Force, XOPE, "Aerospace Expeditionary Force," Detail Concept Paper, Washington, D.C., January 3, 2000.

Headquarters U.S. Air Force, XPMR, The TFA Annexes, file FAM ANNEX Master-26 Sep 00.doc, Washington, D.C., September 26, 2000a.

_____, "The TFA Overarching Guidance," file TFA OG 30 Oct.doc, Washington, D.C., October 30, 2000b.

_____, SSC Dynamic Commitment Vignettes data, file RAND.mdb, Washington, D.C., August 6, 2001.

Headquarters U.S. Air Force, XPPE, PA and PD data from AF Program Data System (PDS): PA (USAF Program, Aerospace Vehicles and Flying Hours) and PD (USAF Program, Bases, Units and Priorities), FY2002 President's Budget, Washington, D.C., July 1, 2001.

Headquarters U.S. Air Force, *Operation Plan and Concept Plan Development and Implementation*, Air Force Instruction 10-401, Vol. I, Washington, D.C., May 1, 1998.

_____, *Manpower & Quality Readiness and Contingency Management*, Air Force Instruction 38-205, Washington, D.C., April 1, 1999a.

_____, *Aerospace Expeditionary Force Planning*, Air Force Instruction 10-400, Washington, D.C., October 1, 1999b.

_____, *Programming USAF Manpower*, Air Force Instruction 38-204, Washington, D.C., October 1, 1999c.

Hitz, Gary, and Don Cohen, "Posturing UTCs and AFWUS Coding," briefing, HQ USAF/XOXW, Washington, D.C., July 17, 2001.

Peck, BGen Al, "CSAF Quarterly Update," briefing, AEF Center, Langley AFB, Va., October 1, 2001.